# THE
# VEGETABLE
# GROWER'S
# DIRECTORY

# THE VEGETABLE GROWER'S DIRECTORY

## A comprehensive guide to growing vegetables and herbs

SUSAN
CONDER

Macdonald

For A.F.C.

A. Macdonald BOOK

© Robert Adkinson Ltd 1986

First published in Great Britain in 1986
by Macdonald & Co (Publishers) Ltd
London & Sydney

A member of BPCC plc

British Library Cataloguing in Publication Data

Conder, Susan
 The vegetable grower's directory.
 1. Vegetable gardening
 I. Title
 635      SB322

 ISBN 0-356-12570-X

Filmset by Dorchester Typesetting Group, Dorchester

Colour origination by La Cromolito, Milan

Printed and bound by Sagdos, Milan


**Designed and produced by Robert Adkinson Ltd, London**
**Editorial Director**
Clare Howell
**Art Director**
Christine Simmonds
**Editor**
Lucy Trench
**Designer**
Chris Warner
**Illustrator**
Julie Stiles


Macdonald & Co (Publishers) Ltd
Greater London House
Hampstead Road
London NW1 7QX

# CONTENTS

# FOREWORD

When confronted with the dozens of books on vegetable growing for sale in book shops or garden centres, it is easy to become overwhelmed. Too much information can be as counterproductive as too little, especially if you see growing vegetables and herbs as a pleasant pastime rather than an all-consuming passion.

*The Vegetable Grower's Directory* is an accessible, but thorough and up-to-date, guide to the subject. Entries in the vegetable and herb sections are arranged in alphabetical order for easy access to information. Basic techniques, such as sowing, planting, watering, feeding and weed control are covered in detail in the introduction, to avoid the endless repetition that is the bane of so many gardening books. Full-colour illustrations identify the major types of each vegetable and herb. If a vegetable is particularly difficult to grow, the text says so, and varieties are included on the basis of ease of cultivation, availability or outstanding flavour. (Gone are the endless lists of varieties, which read like telephone directories and are peppered with obscure, if not unobtainable, entries.)

Simple line drawings convey additional information about techniques and processes particularly relevant to each crop, and a glossary demystifies the most commonly used gardening terms. Also, a calendar clarifies the annual vegetable-growing cycle and puts into perspective what is urgent and what can be left for a while.

The book is small enough for you to take to a garden centre or keep in your pocket while gardening, and pretty enough to make using it a pleasure. Yet for all that, it treats the subject seriously, and assumes a reasonable committment on the part of the reader.

# INTRODUCTION

The ideal spot for a vegetable garden is open and sunny, but also sheltered. Avoid overhanging trees which create shade and compete with crops for soil nutrients and water. As a rough guide, the roots of a tree extend outwards as far as the spread of the branches, although the greedy roots of poplar and willow can spread a great deal further. Avoid, too, nearby tall buildings or narrow, open-ended ground between two buildings. Both can suffer from destructive wind-tunnel effects as well as from shade. (Some vegetables and herbs like light shade, especially in the summer months, but deep shade is definitely a handicap.)

In an exposed garden a windbreak, placed against the prevailing wind, is useful; it can provide shelter for a distance roughly equal to ten times the height. Windbreaks, however, can also overshadow, and if made of quick-growing trees or hedges, can compete with the vegetables at the same time as sheltering them. Stone and brick walls are lovely, but extremely expensive to build. Additionally, solid windbreaks can cause eddies and wind turbulence on the leeward side, so filtering the wind is generally thought to be more effective. Woven wooden fencing or synthetic windbreak netting are realistic and reasonably priced solutions.

Avoid low-lying spots, which tend to be frost pockets or waterlogged or both. Easy access to water, however, is absolutely vital, and if the vegetable garden is near the kitchen and the compost heap as well, it is ideal.

It is simply a matter of opinion whether the sight of the vegetable garden from the house is an eyesore or a source of pride. If you do wish to conceal the vegetables, very attractive screens can be formed from cordon or espaliered fruit trees, or from evergreen honeysuckle trained over a fence.

The traditional vegetable garden is rectangular, about 5m (5½ yds) wide and several times as long. The size and shape of yours will depend on the size and shape of your garden, and what proportion you wish to give to lawns, ornamental plants, children's play area and paved sitting out areas. It also depends on the time you are prepared to give vegetables, the size and tastes of your family, and the importance you attach to self-sufficiency. On a very small scale, vegetables can also be grown in containers on a sheltered balcony or in a courtyard, or as ornamental plants, edging flower beds with red-leaved lettuce or beetroot for example.

Most people, though, find it easier to grow vegetables in beds devoted to that purpose. Traditionally, permanent crops are grown along one edge, with annual and biennial vegetables grown in straight rows, lengthwise or crosswise. (Tall-growing crops, such as runner beans and Jerusalem artichokes, are often sited where they will cast the least shade; or alternated from one year to the next on the long edges of a rectangular plot.) Ideally, rows should run from north to south so the vegetables are evenly exposed to the sun. In fact, a vegetable garden is more usually sited in relation to the rest of the garden – especially if it is small – and the rows simply run parallel to the long or short edges.

With space at a premium many gardeners dispense with rows altogether, spacing vegetables instead the same narrow distance apart in each direction. This 'block' growing of vegetables only works in relatively narrow beds, say 1-1.5m (3-5 ft) across, with access from both sides. The vegetables can be serviced from the paths so no additional space is needed.

Having established the site of the vegetable garden, your next jobs are to make it weed free, free draining and fertile with copious supplies of well rotted organic matter.

## Soil types and improvement

Loam, clay, sand and chalk are the four basic soil types, with many variations between. Each has advantages; some have disadvantages as well, but these can usually be corrected and a wide range of vegetables grown.

Loam, rich in humus, is the easiest soil to work with. (If your soil is loose when dry and can be moulded into a non-sticky ball when wet, it is loam. Colour is another indication, for the darker the soil, the richer in humus it tends to be.) Because the particles of organic and inorganic matter vary in size, loam is generally free draining and well aerated, which is beneficial as plants' roots need air to operate. Paradoxically, loam is also moisture retentive. Even loam, however, can be worn out unless it is given regular supplies of well rotted organic matter.

Clay soil is often rich in nutrients, but impossible to work when wet or dry. Wet clay becomes waterlogged and forms a sticky, solid mass. When dry, it bakes totally hard like concrete. Both of these problems occur because the particles that make up clay are minute: 0.0025mm (0.0001in) or less in diameter. Again, well rotted organic matter is the key. It opens up the texture of the soil, making it more free draining when wet and more moisture retentive when dry. Lime is sometimes used to improve the texture of clay, but adding lime to strongly alkaline soils (see below) does more harm than good. Hopelessly waterlogged clay soils may need to be drained, but the mechanics of land drains are beyond the scope of this book. Never work a waterlogged clay soil as it becomes airless and compact, like potters' clay.

Sandy soil is usually free draining, often too free draining. Not only does it dry out quickly in spring and summer but the nutrients are also drained, or leached, away, making sandy soil a lean, hungry one. On the other hand, sandy soils can be worked at any time of the year and tend to warm up earlier than clay soils in spring.

Increasing the humus content of sandy soil helps retain moisture and also replaces some of the nutrients leached away. Vegetables grown on sandy soil will need more frequent watering and feeding than those grown on heavier soils. Mulching with well rotted organic matter is particularly vital for sandy soils, helping to retain soil moisture in dry weather.

Lastly, chalk soils. Some have a high clay content and are sticky so behave much like clay. Most chalk soils are free draining, and, like sandy soils, have their nutrients continually leached out. Digging in organic matter improves moisture retention and provides some nutrients; it also helps counteract the high alkalinity associated with chalk soils.

Very much related to the type of soil, and to the subsoil underneath, is its acidity. This is measured on a pH scale which ranges from 0-14. Neutral is 7; above 7 is alkaline and below 7 is acid. The ideal pH for most crops is 6.5-7.0 but excesses and deficiencies can usually be corrected.

Use an inexpensive soil-testing kit, available from garden centres and many chemists, to measure your soil's pH. Acidity tends to build up in old or intensely cropped garden soils. To correct excessive acidity, apply lime, either quick-acting hydrated lime or slower acting, but better for the soil, ground limestone. The actual amount varies according to the type of lime used, the degree of acidity and the soil type, but it usually ranges from 150 to 675g per sq m (6 to 24oz per sq yd). Apply it to the soil surface during winter, at least a month after enriching the soil; liming and enriching the soil at the same time are chemically counter productive.

A few types of soil, such as those overlying chalk, are too alkaline. The best long-term remedy is to incorporate well rotted organic matter with moss peat into the soil annually. As a short-term measure, flowers of sulphur can be applied to the soil, at the rate of 100g per sq m (4oz per sq yd).

## Organic fertilizers

Technically, organic fertilizers are those that are natural in origin, derived from plant or animal matter. Using bulky organic matter, such as well rotted manure or garden compost, is a way of adding nutrients to the soil. However, the exact amount of nitrogen, phosphorous and potash, and the trace elements, if any, are never totally predictable. Also, the nutrients contained in bulky organic matter are not readily available to the plants. They have to be broken down by the soil organisms first and are released slowly over a long period of time.

The main reason for using bulky organic fertilizers is to improve the structure of the soil. By increasing its humus content, the soil's aeration and drainage are improved, whether the soil is a heavy or light one. As a general rule, dig in a barrow load per square metre (or yard) in late autumn or early winter. Tradition plays a large part in gardening routines, and well rotted horse manure is the traditional choice for bulky organic matter. In practice, it is difficult to obtain and has almost reached black-market status in some urban areas. Well rotted garden compost, its decomposition hastened by an activator, is the modern equivalent. There are inexpensive, inoffensive, composting bins on the market, useful for small quantities. Lawn mowings,

# INTRODUCTION

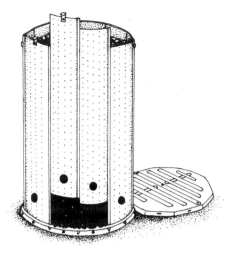

Compost bin

non-woody prunings and bonfire or kitchen waste can be added, but no meat or dairy products, which tend to attract flies and rodents.

If you have enough room and a large enough source of raw material you can build a compost heap; the ideal size is 1.2m (4ft) wide, deep and high. Larger than this, it becomes difficult to ventilate. Compost heaps need ventilation to allow the millions of micro-organisms that break down the raw compost to live. Elevate the heap off the ground by using a layer of well-spaced bricks, woody prunings or upside-down tough plastic perforated seed trays.

Make the sides strong enough to remain rigid. You can use sturdy posts and wire netting, but slatted wooden sides with generous ventilation gaps are better. Wood retains the heat, too, and heat is as important as ventilation. A temperature of 60°C (140°F) is necessary to destroy weed seeds and this heat should be generated during the decomposition process.

Moisture is the third vital factor. Enough water is contained in the raw material and too much can ruin the heap. Keep it covered against rain with corrugated iron, a slatted wooden lid or black plastic held down with planks or bricks.

Compost heap

Alternatives, albeit expensive, include various processed animal manures. These are heat treated to remove pests, diseases and weed seeds; they are also concentrated, de-odorized and generally made clean to handle. Spent mushroom compost, if locally available, is a good bulky fertilizer, though it may be chalky and need to be mixed with more acid organic matter.

Leafmould is excellent. The best is made from oak or beech leaves; those of plane trees and evergreens take too long to break down. Leafmould is also a bit risky. If collected from roadsides it may contain salt, grit and car oil. If collected from woodlands, it may well contain honey fungus. Proceed with caution.

Spent hops and hop haulm can be bought direct from farms or breweries, or, more expensively, in a processed form with the nutrient content increased. Some local councils sell processed sewage (the Chinese have been enriching agricultural land with human waste products for thousands of years). Seaweed is another traditional soil enricher.

Non-bulky organic fertilizers include bone meal and the more finely ground bone flour, used for their phosphate content; hoof and horn, and dried blood, used for their nitrate content; and fish meal, for nitrates and phosphates. In addition, powdered and liquid fertilizers are made from seaweed and other organic extracts.

## Inorganic fertilizers

Although some people feel strongly about the ecological merits of organic fertilizers over inorganic, or chemical, ones, once the nutrients are dissolved in the soil water, a plant can't tell the difference. It *is* true that inorganic fertilizers do nothing to improve the long-term quality of the soil, and over-use can actually harm it. Ideally, one shouldn't need inorganic fertilizers at all, sufficient nutrients being supplied by a soil regularly enriched with well rotted organic matter over many years. In fact, a good compromise can be reached by digging in as much organic matter as possible and supplementing this with moderate quantities of quick-acting chemical fertilizers.

There are straight and compound chemical fertilizers. The former contain one or largely one of the three main nutrients: nitrogen, for leaf and stem growth; phosphorus, for root growth; and potash, for maintaining growth to maturity and for resistance to disease. Most people, however, rely on compound fertilizers. These contain a balanced combination of the three, as well as various trace elements, such as magnesium and molybdenum, which plants need in tiny quantities. Chemical compound fertilizers for specific plants contain slightly more of one component or another. Tomato fertilizer, for example, is high in potash. The usual combination, though, is 7% nitrogen, 7% phosphorus and 7% potash – the exact analysis should be on the label.

While 'straights' are used to give vegetables a particular boost at a particular time – nitrates, for example, are given to overwintering brassicas at the end of winter to help them begin growth – compound fertilizers are usually raked into the soil a week or two before sowing or planting. Slow maturing crops also benefit from additional feeds of compound fertilizer, once or twice during the growing season, to replace nutrients taken from the soil.

Granular and powder fertilizers, whether organic or inorganic, should be applied on a still day; powders, particularly, sticking to wet foliage can burn it, so keep well away from the top growth. For large gardens, it might be worth investing in a mechanical spreader which scatters the fertilizer evenly. An old-fashioned, but effective, alternative, is to mix the fertilizer with coarse sand.

Liquid fertilizer, whether diluted concentrated liquid or soluble powder, is very fast acting when watered into the soil. (Water the soil first if dry.) Fastest of all is foliar feeding; it is also useful for plants with shallow or relatively small root systems. There are a number of proprietary foliar feeds.

As a general rule, compound fertilizers should be applied at the rate of 60g per sq m (20 oz per sq yd). Never exceed the recommended quantities on the label, and store in a cool, dry place out of reach of children.

## Crop rotation and planning

In the flower garden, most people know that a bed which has grown roses for many years should not be re-planted with new roses; the soil is likely to suffer from rose sickness and the new plants will fail. This, in a nutshell, is the principle behind crop rotation, a subject that has such highly scientific overtones that the mere mention of it is enough to put many people off growing vegetables altogether.

The practice of crop rotation is based on three simple and easily understood ideas. The first is that pests and diseases specific to a particular plant or type of plant, such as brassicas, tend to build up in soil on which those plants are grown year after year. The second is that different plants take different proportions of nutrients from the soil, in varying quantities and from varying levels, depending on whether the plants are shallow or deep rooted. The third is that different vegetables benefit from slightly different types of soil preparation.

Where the analogy between roses and vegetables ends is the time scale. Unlike roses, which are long lived, most vegetables are annuals so are automatically replaced every year. (Permanent vegetables, such as rhubarb, asparagus and globe artichoke, do not form part of the annual crop rotation, but when it is time to replace old, worn-out plants with new ones, a different part of the garden should be used.)

Crop rotation is normally organized on a three-year plan. This entails dividing the vegetable plot into roughly equal thirds; the vegetables are divided into three groups, according to their botanical family connections, such as the brassicas, or according to their habits of growth, such as root vegetables. Each group of vegetables occupies the same piece of land one year out of three. (Crop rotation has nothing to do with the size of a garden, and even small patches benefit from it. It is not relevant, though, to containerized growing for which fresh compost is used every year.)

There are slight variations in the way plants are grouped. Old-fashioned gardeners, for example, often grew onions on a permanent bed, but this is now frowned upon. Most experts agree on the three basic divisions: brassicas; root vegetables; and legumes plus assorted odds and ends. Brassicas include broccoli, Brussels sprouts, cabbage, cauliflower, kale, radish, swede and turnip. (Sometimes, however, the last three are grouped with root vegetables.) Root vegetables normally include beetroot, carrot, chicory, Jerusalem artichoke, parsnip, potato, salsify and scorzonera. The third group, sometimes referred to as the greedy feeders, or the pod, stem and bulb crops, include such legumes as broad beans, French beans, peas and runner beans, as well as aubergines, capsicum, celeriac, celery, cucumber, endive, leek, lettuce, marrow and courgette, onion, spinach, sweetcorn and tomato.

The order in which main groups of vegetables follow one another is determined by the requirements of the crop. Brassicas are not greedy feeders so they do best on firm, neutral or alkaline soil enriched for a previous crop. Brassicas, therefore, normally follow the third group, or greedy feeders, which appreciate generously enriched soil. (The legumes leave nitrogen behind in the soil, an additional bonus for brassicas.) Roots follow brassicas because, again, roots prefer firm, but not heavily enriched soil, and root vegetables can tap minerals and nutrients from lower in the soil than the shallow-rooted brassicas.

Except for the cardinal rule of never following one brassica crop with another, there is a certain amount of lexibility in crop rotation. You may not want, or need, exactly the same proportion of ground devoted to root crops as to brassicas, or may grow no brassicas at all. In that case, aim to alternate deep- and shallow-rooting crops on a two-year basis. You may want to follow early lettuce by carrots or beetroot, instead of a brassica. You may like to intercrop a row of turnips between rows of slower-growing peas, or you may want a quick-growing catch crop of carrots before setting out cabbage plants in late spring. As long as your crops are growing well, it is worth experimenting. If a crop fails though, you must not use that ground for another crop from that group for at least a year.

The smaller your vegetable garden, the more important it is to use every bit of space. Sensible measures to maximize your production include growing dwarf varieties, or tall-growing varieties along walls or fences; selecting fast-growing or high-yielding vegetables; choosing high-yielding varieties; and making full use of containers.

## Equipment

In spite of the saying 'A poor workman blames his tools', inferior tools and equipment *are* detrimental to the job in hand, whether gardening or anything else. Buy the best basic tools you can afford, not a plethora of bargain-priced gadgets.

Polished stainless steel tools are very expensive but long-lasting, lightweight, and easier to use and clean because of the reduced soil adhesion. Good quality, reliable tools can be had in hot-forged carbon steel, often with a hammer finish to resist corrosion. Some manufacturers do a decent budget-range in hot-forged carbon steel, but beware of thin, pressed steel which is short-lived and easily bent.

You need a digging spade or, if you prefer, a slightly smaller border spade, which used to be called a lady's spade before the days of equality between the sexes. Likewise, you need a four-tined digging fork, or its slightly smaller version, the border fork. Choose spades and forks with weatherproof polypropylene handles and tough ashwood shafts, ideally sheathed in PVC or wax impregnated for added protection. Flat-tined potato forks are very much optional extras.

Buy a square, rigid garden rake, not a fan-shaped, flexible lawn rake. The best have stainless steel heads

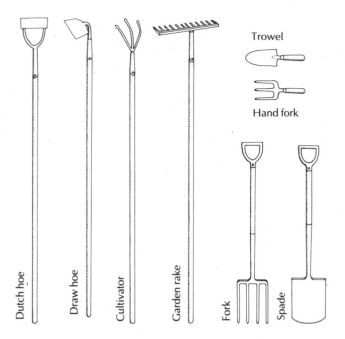

Trowel

Hand fork

Dutch hoe

Draw hoe

Cultivator

Garden rake

Fork

Spade

and aluminium shafts with full-length PVC sleeves. Medium-priced rakes have heat-treated, epoxy-coated carbon steel heads and epoxy-coated aluminium shafts. There are acceptable budget rakes with painted carbon steel heads, and epoxy-coated tubular steel shafts.

There are three types of hoe. A Dutch hoe has a stirrup-shaped blade that is pushed forward through the soil. A traditional draw hoe, drawn through the soil, has a rectangular, triangular or semi-circular blade at right angles to the shaft. (The onion hoe is a small version of a draw hoe, and is useful in tight spots.) The modern, proprietary cultivator has three working edges to its elongated triangular head. If you are only buying one, buy the draw, or possibly proprietary, hoe. Quality and components vary as for rakes.

Hand trowels and hand forks are vital, especially for containerized vegetable growing. The best have stainless steel heads and lacquered beechwood handles; less expensive, but acceptable, models have epoxy-coated, heat-treated carbon steel heads. Long-handled trowels can be awkward to use; narrow, pointed trowels are useful for small-scale work.

# EQUIPMENT

Watering by hand is only practical in the very smallest of vegetable gardens. Choose a watering can that is well balanced and not too heavy to carry when full; 7-9l (1½-2 gal) capacity should be alright. Polythene watering cans are shorter-lived than metal ones, but are inexpensive and, with reasonable care, last for several years. Buy two heads, or roses: a fine one for watering seedlings and a coarse one for general-purpose watering.

A hose with an adjustable nozzle makes much lighter work of watering. The best hoses are double-walled and reinforced; they are long lasting and do not kink but are expensive. A good-quality plastic hose should suffice for most gardeners. Any hose is easier to use and store with a reel. Easiest of all to use is perforated tubing which releases a slow trickle of water at regular intervals.

A garden knife with a tungsten or carbon steel blade is useful, as long as it is regularly sharpened. Secateurs, or pruners, are also useful. Choose those with a double-cut – sometimes called 'parrot-beak' – action, rather than the anvil type with one cutting edge. A pair of good scissors for harvesting herbs and easily damaged vegetables is also handy.

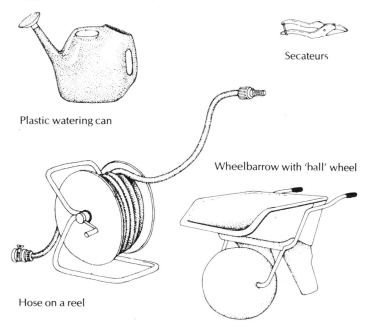

Secateurs

Plastic watering can

Wheelbarrow with 'ball' wheel

Hose on a reel

# INTRODUCTION

Wheelbarrows are either of galvanized steel or polypropylene, fitted wth rubber tyres or inflated balls. Steel wheelbarrows are longer lasting but more expensive than polypropylene ones. Those fitted with balls spread the load over a larger area and consequently don't sink into wet soil. Wheelbarrows come in various sizes; make sure the one you choose is not too big for you, and that the weight is carried over the ball or wheel, not over the handles. Some have top extensions for bulky loads.

Smaller, but still useful, items include garden string, sprayers for pesticides and fungicides, dibbers for planting out and labels for marking rows.

## Protection

In cool temperate climates, every extra frost-free day wrested from nature is a bonus. Both in terms of getting a head start with the spring outdoor sowing and planting, or protecting fully grown and cropping plants from the first autumn frost, artificial protection can mean the difference between a non-existent crop and a successful, bountiful one.

The ever-inventive Victorians invented bell jars, made of thick glass with a knob at the top for lifting. Such jars are rare today, and have made the transition from lowly garden equipment to antiques. Though you can buy individual, clear PVC plant covers with ventilation holes, you can also make your own by cutting the bottom off a large, clear plastic container, such as that used for squash. Large plastic fizzy-drink bottles are ideal; some have fully rounded, blow-moulded plastic bases kept stable by an outer, flat plastic 'cup'. Cut off the top, prize the outer 'cup' off, and you have a contemporary bell jar. Collect glass jam and coffee jars; each one can protect a seedling from the ravages of wind and rain as well as frost.

Cloches offer larger-scale continuous protection. The main choice is between glass and plastic. Glass is longer lasting, more retentive of heat, and remains clear. It is less likely to blow over than plastic. On the other hand, it is expensive, needs careful handling and can be dangerous, especially if there are young children around. Storage, too, can be a problem. Plastic is safe and inexpensive, but short lived, retains less heat and may turn opaque with age.

Tent cloche

Barn cloche

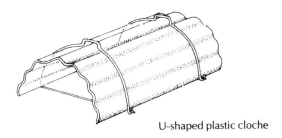

U-shaped plastic cloche

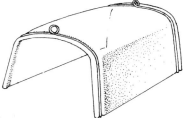

Tunnel cloche

# INTRODUCTION

As well as materials, there is a wide choice of shapes.
Tent cloches, for low-growing plants, are triangular in
section. Barn cloches have sides slightly angled inwards
and pitched roofs. Low barn cloches are about 30cm
(12in) high at the ridge; high barn cloches are about
45cm (18in) high. Utility cloches are made of three rigid
panes wired together. There are tunnel cloches made of
rigid currogated PVC held in place with wire, and
semi-transparent U-shaped plastic cloches.

Flexible cloches include the traditional polythene
sheeting over wire hoops, and the newer double-
skinned cloching, made of a plastic-covered or galvanized
mesh frame covered on both sides with polythene.
Newer still is growing film, which is clear, perforated
plastic film spread loosely over the seedling crop, with
the ends tucked into the soil. As the crops grow, the slits
open, allowing more air and water to get to the crops.

You can improvise with commercially produced
cloches. For extra height around one plant, place two
barn cloches on end, enclosing the plant. Firmly fix with
canes attached to the wires and pushed into the soil.

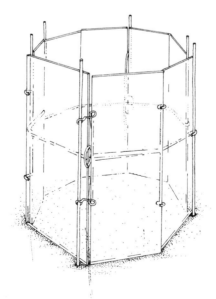

Two barn cloches on end

22

# PROTECTION

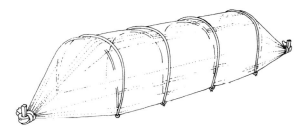

Cloche of polythene sheeting over wire hoops

Knowing when to take cloches off is as important as knowing when to put them on. Cloches put on a week or two before sowing or planting can warm up the soil temperature considerably. Once the danger of frost is over, however, life inside a cloche can become intolerably hot and plants can literally steam to death. The warmer it is, the more ventilation will be necessary and increased ventilation has the additional purpose of hardening off plants before the cloches are removed. Leave spaces between cloches to ventilate; leaving the ends open creates a wind tunnel. There is no need to remove cloches for watering.

There are old-fashioned emergency measures against frost, worth reviving. Cover young plants or seedlings with a 5cm (2in) layer of light, dry, leaf litter, newspaper, straw or conifer branches when night frost threatens, and remove them the next morning. Covering cloches with sacks or matting against sudden, severe frost is also a sensible precaution.

# INTRODUCTION

## Sowing seed indoors

Like new-born babies, infant plants need the best possible conditions if they are to remain healthy and strong. Don't sow too early; instead of a head start, you'll be making a false start. The seedlings will grow quickly and be ready for moving outdoors before temperatures allow. Unless you have a huge greenhouse, the plants will be crowded together for weeks on end, so vulnerable to pests and diseases. Follow the timing suggested on the seed packet, making minor adjustments if your garden is particularly mild and sheltered, or exposed and cold.

Seeds refuse to germinate above or below certain temperatures. The cut-off points vary from vegetable to vegetable, but generally, temperatures between 10-21°C (50-70°F) are adequate. Most people err on the side of heat, out of a misplaced sense of kindness, or to speed things up. Seedlings raised in cool conditions are tougher and healthier.

You can buy propagators, both heated and unheated, but they aren't necessary. Any shallow, free-draining and meticulously clean container will do. (Previously used clay pots should be sterilized first with diluted Jeyes fluid. Plastic pots and trays need thorough washing.) Peat pots have revolutionized sowing techniques. Both hollow peat pots, filled with a standard seed compost or expandible jiffy pots, can be planted directly into the soil, with no disturbance to the plants' roots. On the other hand, they need very careful watering.

Use fresh seed compost; peat-based is generally easier than soil-based. Fill the container nearly to the top, then firm gently with a flat board or your fingers. Moisten the compost with a watering can fitted with a fine rose, or a fine mist sprayer filled with water.

Sow the seed thinly. Pelleted and naturally large seeds, such as those of the cucurbit family, can be 'station' sown. Mix smaller seed with a bit of fine silver sand and, using your thumb and forefinger, scatter pinches over the surface of the compost. Do not cover fine seed; larger seeds should be covered with a layer of sifted compost equal to their own thickness.

If using a propagator, replace the lid and place in a shady spot. Enclosing pots in clear polythene bags has much the same effect; again, keep shaded initially. Alternatively, cover the containers with a sheet of glass

# SOWING SEED INDOORS

Propagator

Heated propagator

Plastic and clay pots
and a seed tray

Peat pots

Jiffy pots

Levelling off the
seed compost

Watering the
seed tray

Sowing the seed

Covering the seeds with compost

A pane of glass over the seed tray

Pricking out seedlings

Planting seedlings

topped with brown paper to exclude light. A humid –
not dank – atmosphere is needed, so wipe off any
condensation that forms on the lid, polythene bag or
glass. Additional watering is not usually necessary.

Inspect the compost regularly; as soon as the
seedlings are visible, gradually expose them to bright
but indirect light. Gradually expose them to normal
atmospheric conditions as well, opening the vents of the
propagator lid, propping up panes of glass, or
perforating the polythene bag. After three or four days,
remove protection completely. Water as necessary to
keep the compost damp.

As soon as the seedlings are large enough to handle –
when either the seed leaves or the first pair of true leaves
have formed – prick them out into trays or pots, using a
soil- or peat-based potting compost. Hold the seedlings
by their leaves, levering them out with a plastic seed
label, spoon handle or even ice-lolly stick. Use a pencil
to make holes for the roots, spaced 2.5-4cm (1-1½in)
apart, then insert the seedlings and firm the compost.
Water lightly and keep shaded for a day or two.

Seedlings of plants intended for the garden should
gradually be exposed to lower temperatures and
increased ventilation. This is done initially indoors, but
eventually put the young plants out on sunny days,
bringing them in at night or when frost threatens.

## Sowing seed outdoors

Quick-growing crops, and root crops which don't
transplant well, are usually sown where they are to
grow. Slower-growing vegetables, such as many
brassicas, are usually sown in seed or nursery beds, then
transplanted to their final positions at a later date.
Using a seed bed frees valuable space in a small garden
and reduces the scale of such routine chores as weeding
and watering. Some plants benefit from being
transplanted deeper than they originally grew.

Whether the seed is sown in a temporary or
permanent bed, it should be well prepared. Ideally, the
ground should be dug over, weeded and enriched in the
autumn or winter before sowing, then left rough over
winter, exposed to the elements. The second stage, or
final preparation, usually takes place in early spring, but
be guided by your own soil and the weather. Sowing too

# SOWING SEED OUTDOORS

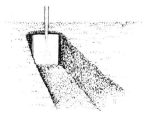

Digging a trench in autumn

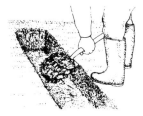

Adding well rotted compost

Digging the next trench

Levelling off the trench

Breaking up the soil in spring

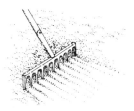

Levelling the soil

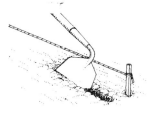

Making a drill with a draw hoe

Making a broad drill

Sowing the seed

Levelling off

early on a heavy, wet, clay soil; or on any soil if early spring is unseasonably cold, ensures failure. (The traditional rule of thumb, or rule of foot, says that if the soil sticks to your boots, postpone finishing the seed bed.)

A week or two before the intended sowing date, use a garden fork to break up the large clods of soil. Remove stones, leaves, garden rubble and any weeds that may have germinated. Roughly level the soil and rake in a general-purpose fertilizer. Covering the soil with cloches at this stage helps to warm it up.

Immediately before sowing, lightly tread the soil to firm it, then use a rake to achieve an even, level surface. An uneven seed bed means that seeds will be sown at uneven depths and losses will result. The old-fashioned phrase 'Rake to a fine tilth' means that the soil should have a crumb-like texture to a depth of about 2.5cm (1in); the finer the seed, the more important a good tilth is.

Drills – straight, shallow depressions in the soil – are usually spaced 15cm (6in) apart in seed beds; in a permanent bed they are placed according to vegetable. Drills are generally 15mm (½in) deep. They can be slightly shallower for very small seed and on very heavy soils; deeper for large seed and on light, free-draining soils. Use a taut line to mark the rows, and use the side of a draw hoe, or a rake or hoe handle pressed firmly into the soil, to make the drill. For broad drills, such as those for peas, use the whole blade of a spade or draw hoe. If the soil is dry, water using a hose with the nozzle adjusted to give a fine spray, or a watering can fitted with a fine rose.

Sow large or pelleted seed individually, spaced well apart. Sow smaller seed thinly, releasing it between the thumb and forefinger. As with seed sown under glass, very fine seed should be coated with silver sand first, or possibly mixed with radish seed. After sowing, cover the seeds with soil, by hand or using the back of a rake.

If the seeds involved are large and the number of plants relatively few – marrows or ridge cucumbers, for example – use a trowel or wooden dibber to make individual holes. Although some vegetables have a higher germination rate than others, germination is never one hundred per cent. Sow two or three seeds in each position, then thin to the strongest if necessary.

# Watering

Like people, most of a vegetable's weight is water. Like people, vegetables 'perspire' when hot to keep cool. (The process of losing water through the leaves is technically known as transpiration.) Unlike people, vegetables can only take their nutrients in liquid form. Although sometimes foliar feeds are used, most of a plant's food comes through its roots, which means that soil moisture must be present for plants to eat.

In the wild, plants are suited naturally to the amount of water available. Highly bred vegetable cultivars are a long way from home, both geographically and genetically, so they usually need artificial watering in the summer months.

Unfortunately, there is no hard and fast rule as to how much watering is required. Free-draining soils, such as sandy ones or thin soils overlying chalk, can hold less water and therefore dry out quicker than heavy clay or loam soils. Digging in well rotted organic matter, to help retain soil moisture, is vital for such dry soils and reduces the need for continual watering.

Vegetables growing in full sun or windy sites dry out more quickly than those growing in shade and shelter, and vegetables growing in high temperatures obviously need more moisture than those growing in cool ones. Vegetables with thin leaves, shallow or small root systems, and those that are quick growing, need more water than those that are slow growing, have thick leaves and deep or large root systems. Containerized plants need more frequent watering than those in the open ground.

At certain times of their lives, vegetables are very vulnerable to drying out. Seedlings and newly potted on or transplanted plants are prime candidates. Before sowing or planting outdoors, water the ground thoroughly so the top 15-20cm (6-8in) of soil is damp; you can check this with a spade.

When vegetables are flowering (*not* bolting), setting or swelling, they need steady, generous supplies of water. Insufficient water results in bud drop and crop losses. Irregular watering causes the roots, bulbs or stem bases, and fruits to split. Once vegetables are full sized, watering should be decreased, then stopped.

Whenever watering, make sure the soil surface is open enough for the water to penetrate. A hard, compacted soil surface is virtually waterproof and the water simply runs off. Hoe a caked surface first to break it up. The worst way to water is too little and too often. This teases the plants' roots, encouraging shallow rooting and making them doubly vulnerable to the next drought. As a general guide, allow for 9l per sq m (2 gal per sq yd) at least once a week in dry weather.

Water, if possible, in early morning; the mid-day sun can scorch wet vegetables. In the evening, falling temperatures combined with wet conditions encourage various fungal infections. Applying a mulch to thoroughly wet soil does help conserve soil moisture and keep the plants' roots cool.

Finally, an old-fashioned trick is to sink a flower pot up to its rim in the soil next to individual plants: tomatoes, green peppers, melons or cucumbers, for example. In addition to general watering, filling the pots with water ensures a steady supply to the roots.

## Weed control

A weed is a plant growing in the wrong place. Self-sown seedlings of lemon balm; potatoes left in the ground after harvesting that sprout the following spring; or a clump of sorrel encroaching on other vegetables are as much weeds as thistles, nettles and ground elder. Weeds compete with crops for space, sunlight, nutrients and moisture. Weeds also provide a home for pests and diseases, and give a garden an unkempt look.

With weed control a stitch in time saves nine. Removing all visible perennial weeds when digging over the soil in autumn, and deeply burying annual ones, as green manure, helps. Unfortunately, it is not a total solution. Seeds, particularly of annual weeds, are inevitably contained in the soil and will germinate when the weather warms up. Perennial weeds, such as couch grass, are more difficult. Tiny little snippets left in the soil are capable of sending out new roots and leaves.

For those with large, totally weed-infested vegetable gardens, renting a rotavator is an option. Used several times during the course of a growing season, the machine eventually wears out the weed population by disturbing the soil and physically uprooting and damaging the weeds. It is, however, an expensive and time-consuming approach, and a whole growing season is lost.

An easier, and more modern method, is to use a chemical weedkiller before sowing or planting. Glyphosate is a total weedkiller. Selective weedkillers include 2, 4, 5, T, which eradicates tough, woody weeds, thistles and nettles; and dalapon which kills annual and perennial grasses. Use all weedkillers according to the manufacturer's recommendations, and set aside a clearly marked watering can for that purpose.

No matter how meticulous your preparation, there will be weeds growing in among crops. Hoeing between rows and hand weeding between plants is the traditional solution. You can hoe between plants, but there is a danger of damaging the stems and roots. You can spray or paint individual, particularly difficult weeds with a proprietory mixture of paraquat and diquat. Some people use flame guns to destroy weeds between rows of vegetables, but great care has to be taken not to damage nearby crops.

Mulching with well rotted compost or straw, or covering the soil with black polythene sheeting, smothers all but the most tenacious weeds. To use polythene, water the soil first if it is dry, then lay the sheeting, burying the edges in the ground. Make slits at the correct spacing and insert young plants through them, or, more simply, lay the sheeting between rows.

Separating seedling vegetables from seedling weeds can be difficult. Some seed packets illustrate the seedling vegetables so you can identify them. There is a pre-emergent weedkiller, propachlor, which prevents weed seeds germinating for about six weeks. However, it can only be used with certain crops, such as brassicas, onions and leeks.

Finally, don't put perennial weeds or flowering or seeding annual weeds on the compost heap. Ideally, the heat generated in the compost heap should kill weeds and seeds, but they often do germinate and grow. Put them on the bonfire instead.

## Container growing

It is both harder and easier to grow vegetables in containers than in the open ground. You may, however, have no option but to use your balcony, terrace or

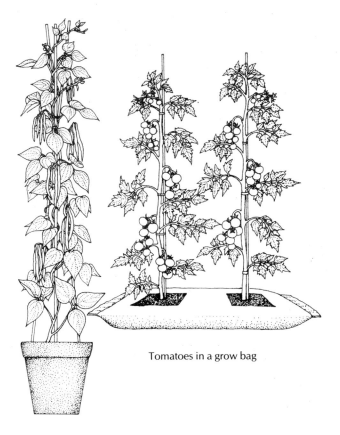

Tomatoes in a grow bag

Beans growing in a pot

concrete patch. If that is the case, remember that the plants are likely to be seen from the house, so choose vegetables such as dwarf beans and tomatoes that are pretty as well as edible.

Container-grown vegetables can be moved around to follow the sun, or placed indoors to avoid frosts. Remember that outdoor containers need shelter and protection from the fierce summer sun.

Container growing involves frequent, immaculately controlled watering, often twice a day in the hot summer months. Over-watering, however, can be fatal, especially for plants in peat-based composts. The roots of container-grown vegetables are more vulnerable to frost and baking heat than they are in the open ground, which acts as insulation.

On the other hand, using sterilized loam- or peat-based compost means that soil-borne pests and diseases are virtually non-existent, and weeding rarely necessary. Never use garden soil for container growing. It is unlikely to contain the right balance of nutrients and may have weed seeds, pests and diseases. Garden soil also tends to compact into a solid block.

Although there are all manner of coy and eccentric containers, there is nothing as good as a flower pot. Nicest looking are the terracotta ones, though they are expensive and hard to clean. Still, they can be treated as long-term investments. Plastic pots are lightweight, cheap, easy to clean and need less frequent watering than clay ones. On the other hand, they can be knocked over easily, especially if filled with lightweight, peat-based compost. Whether plastic or terracotta, pots should have a minimum depth of 20cm (8in); in most pots, the depth equals the diameter at the rim.

Grow bags are very convenient, but rather an eyesore in the garden. The vegetables can be supported either by special supports which fit in the bags, or by bamboo canes, or by wire and trellis on a nearby wall.

Peat-based compost is lightweight and 'clean', but has less nutrient content than loam-based compost and needs frequent watering. If it dries out completely, you may very well lose the plant. Loam-based compost can take a less scientific watering regime, has a longer-lasting supply of nutrients, and is heavier, so counter-balancing tall, heavy crops such as tomatoes.

If using peat-based compost and plastic pots, no crocking is necessary. Otherwise, make a 2.5cm (1in) layer of drainage material, such as pebbles or broken clay flower pots, in the bottom of the pot. Though not strictly necessary, a layer of fine mesh over the crocking prevents compost seeping down through the drainage material, and prevents any insect pests entering through the drainage holes to attack the plant's roots. The compost should come 2.5cm (1in) below the level of the rim to allow for watering.

As well as most of the herbs, there are many dwarf varieties of vegetables ideal for container growing. And, of course, vegetables grown quickly and harvested when young, such as early carrots and turnips, are ideal.

# VEGETABLES

There is something very satisfying about growing your own food. It may be that beneath our civilized, suburbanized or urbanized exteriors lurks a vestigial primitive instinct to provide food for survival. Nevermind that a nearby supermarket is an instant source of supplies; the pride in growing your own still remains.

From the daily inspection of a seed tray for the first sign of life, to picking runner beans on a summer's evening (perhaps with a sherry balanced on the ground nearby), the processes of cultivating and harvesting crops are as enjoyable as eating them. Home freezers solve much of the problem of bumper crops and extend the enjoyment into the winter months.

On a more mundane level, working in the vegetable garden is usually a solitary process, away from everyone else and the niggling domestic committments of everyday life. And because many of the tasks are repetitive – even mindless – you can often think of other things while you work, letting your mind wander where it will.

Vegetables grown for home consumption need not meet the rigorous – even fanatical – standards of those grown for exhibition or commerce. The Victorians, for example, in their quest for perfection, devised glass cylinders to enclose developing cucumbers. The latter had no option but to mature literally perfectly straight, and without the tiniest disfigurement. Those who grow for exhibition today continue that tradition. There are books devoted to exhibition growing; the secrets of feeding marrows and pumpkins until they are bloated beyond all natural limits, are handed down from generation to generation. For the perfectionist a single superb specimen is the ultimate goal.

For the commercial grower, quantity becomes far more important and methods often differ from those suitable in small gardens. Varieties with the heaviest yields, that travel well, keep well, and sell well are preferred to those that are more delicious but perhaps look rather odd in appearance, have lower yields, don't travel well or need special care. Commercial crops are harvested when they weigh most, which may be long after the flavour has peaked and the texture is at its most succulent. Less familiar vegetables, and those with 'foreign' overtones, are usually ignored, and any that do reach the shops are highly priced, however easy they may have been to grow.

As a home grower, you needn't worry about what sells and what doesn't. You needn't worry about the odd blemish or insect, or reaching the exacting standards of size and perfection required for exhibition work. You can grow what you enjoy raising and what you and your family enjoy eating.

Although much is made of the economy of growing your own vegetables, calculations are always based on unpaid labour. And whether it is tending a full-scale allotment, or a few lettuces tucked around the base of rose bushes in a mixed border, it should be seen as a labour of love.

# ARTICHOKES, GLOBE

Globe artichoke is an unusual vegetable because the immature flower buds form the only edible portion. These giant thistles, when allowed to mature and display their bright-blue centres, are much loved by flower arrangers. In fact, the silvery white leaves and large-scale, architectural form of the plant are equally attractive, and it is often grown at the back of herbaceous borders. In the kitchen, it is a fiddly vegetable to prepare and takes a long time to cook, but it is highly regarded by the French, and most gourmets love its subtle-tasting flesh. Eating a globe artichoke is a messy, but pleasant ritual. Each 'leaf' (more correctly, scale) is pulled from the head, dipped in a sauce or dressing then pulled between the teeth to extract the flesh from the leaf base. Finally, the inedible choke is removed with a spoon and the base, or fond, is eaten with a knife and fork.

Globe artichoke

## Site and soil

Globe artichoke is a princess among vegetables; if it can't have shelter, full sun, and a light but rich, well drained soil, it isn't worth growing. In the autumn or winter before planting work in well rotted compost, and immediately before planting sprinkle general-purpose fertilizer on the soil surface.

## Cultivation

Globe artichokes can be grown

from seed, but they take several years to reach maturity. Instead, buy young offsets (rooted cuttings) from a garden centre in mid-spring. Plant 1m (3ft) apart in each direction, then keep weeded and well watered, especially in dry weather. A top dressing of more organic matter, applied in late spring, helps keep weeds down, provides additional nutrition and conserves soil moisture; but make sure the soil is moist before applying this dressing.

The first summer, remove all flower buds as soon as they appear to allow the young plants to build up strength for future cropping. In any case, never let the flowers develop fully and set seed; the plants are weakened, and the flowers tough and inedible.

In autumn, when all the top growth has died down, cut it back to just above ground level. Protect the crowns from frost by covering them with a mound of soil (rather like earthing up potatoes) or a layer of straw, leafmould or well rotted compost, held in place with wire mesh. Remove in mid-spring; if the protective covering is left on too long, the plants beneath may rot.

Like most perennials, globe artichokes deteriorate with time. After three or four years, the flowers become fewer, smaller and tougher. Replace with young, rooted offshoots carefully removed from the base of the plant in mid-spring. Put down slug pellets between the plants as slugs and snails are very fond of the young shoots. Aphids like the tender

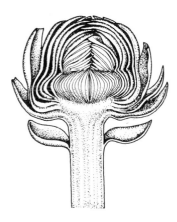

Section through a globe artichoke

Globe artichoke
'Green Globe'

growing tips; spray with an insecticide suitable for crops.

**Harvesting and storing**
A fully mature plant should produce at least ten heads per season. Pick when they are full size, about 10cm (4in) in diameter, but not yet open; this is usually in early or mid-summer. Pick the large head at the end of the flower stalk first. This is called the king head, and its removal encourages the growth of the smaller, side heads lower down the stalk. Using secateurs, leave 2.5cm (1in) of stalk attached to the head and prune the remaining stalk back to just above the next flower bud. Pick the smaller side heads as they mature. Globe artichokes keep up to a week in a refrigerator, after which they tend to dry out and discolour.

**Varieties**
'Green Globe', sometimes sold as 'Green Ball' is the sort usually offered by seed catalogues. It is similar to 'Camus de Bretagne', or 'Grand Camus de Bretagne', and 'Vert de Laon'. All have large green heads but are only moderately hardy. For cold, exposed gardens 'Purple Globe' is a safer bet, though its flavour is said to be inferior.

# ARTICHOKES, JERUSALEM

Jerusalem artichoke

A closer relative of the sunflower than the globe artichoke, Jerusalem artichoke is an extremely hardy perennial grown as an annual. Like potatoes, its tuberous roots are eaten, boiled or roasted. Unlike potatoes, the roots are knobbly, contorted and difficult to peel and, for this reason, not very popular with cooks. It takes the better part of a year from planting to harvesting and, as the plants can grow 3m (10ft) or more in height, Jerusalem artichoke is for the larger garden only.

**Site and soil**
Jerusalem artichoke is traditionally the Cinderella of vegetables, grown in an odd corner of poor, dry soil and totally neglected. Better crops can be had from a rich, free-draining soil (not too acidic), sun and shelter. Digging in well rotted compost in the autumn or winter before planting is beneficial, but not essential.

Although it can act as a windbreak, a row of Jerusalem artichokes also casts a lot of shade when fully grown, so consider carefully what is to grow nearby.

**Cultivation**
Plant egg-size, relatively smooth tubers from late winter onwards. Large tubers can be cut in half. Plant 15cm (6in) deep and 60cm (2ft) apart, in rows 1m (3ft) apart. Alternatively plant the tubers

the same depth and distance apart in a large corner of the garden. In a group, they support each other so staking is not necessary.

Cover the tubers with a slight ridge or mound of soil; germination can take up to a month. Once the young stems are 30cm (12in) high, continue mounding earth round the stems – rather like earthing up potatoes – until a 15cm (6in) high mound is formed. This encourages the production of more, and shallower, tubers, making harvesting easier.

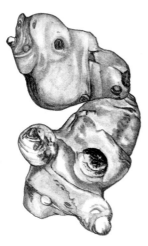

Jerusalem artichoke tubers

Plants grown in rows do need support. Drive 1.8m (6ft) long stakes one third of their height into the ground at the ends of the row, with an intermediate stake if the row is longer than 3.5m (12ft). Connect two wires to the stakes, one at the top and one half-way up, then attach the plants to the wires.

Once the plants reach a height of 1.5m (5ft), clip the growing points off. Water only in very dry weather and put down slug pellets if slugs are troublesome. Bromophos sprinkled over the soil at planting time should discourage cutworms, root aphids, chafer grubs and swift moth larvae if they have been a problem in recent years.

When the leaves start to turn brown in autumn, cut the stems back to 30cm (12in) above ground.

**Harvesting and storing**
Begin harvesting in mid-autumn and continue until the end of winter. Fork well under the root system to get up every tuber; any left in the ground will sprout. Store tubers in the refrigerator or, for longer-term storage, in boxes of peat. If the ground is unlikely to freeze, leave the tubers in the soil and dig up as needed. Save the best tubers for next year's crop.

**Varieties**
With tubers bought from a greengrocer, variety is a moot point. Horticultural suppliers offer either 'Fuseau' or 'New White', both smooth, white-skinned types with a sweet, nutty flavour.

# ASPARAGUS

Asparagus

Asparagus demands a long-term investment of time and space. Most vegetables are annuals, quick to crop but equally quick to die. Asparagus is a hardy herbaceous perennial that takes several seasons to become established and crops for only six weeks a year. Once mature, however, it can crop for twenty-five or more years. It is one of the earliest garden vegetables and one whose flavour is most superb if cooked within a few minutes of being picked. Realistically, it is not worth growing less than a dozen plants.

Asparagus is a member of the lily family, and a cousin of the popular houseplants of the same name. It is the young shoots that are eaten; left to mature, they produce delicate ferny foliage 1.2m (4ft) or more high.

## Site and soil
Sun and shelter are essential. There is an old saying that land good for growing potatoes is good for growing asparagus. Well drained, deep, rich, neutral soil is ideal. Other soils, however, can give good results provided preparation is thorough. The autumn or winter before planting, work in plenty of well rotted compost, remembering that asparagus roots are both deep and wide-spreading. Remove every trace of weed root as you dig; perennial weeds in an asparagus bed are a gardener's

nightmare. On very wet soils asparagus is often grown on raised beds, though opponents point out that, unless a drainage system is installed, some of the roots are still faced with waterlogged soil. Before planting, apply a general-purpose fertilizer.

## Cultivation

Asparagus can be grown from seed, but this is a waste of at least a year's time and the quality of plants grown from seed varies. Instead, buy one-year-old crowns; two- and three-year-old crowns are sometimes available, but they are more difficult to get established. (Some seed merchants also supply young crowns.)

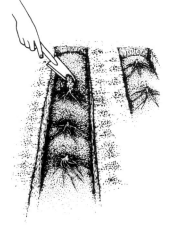

Asparagus roots spread out in a trench

In mid-spring dig a trench on the prepared ground, one spade deep and 30cm (12in) wide. Return some of the soil, making a 10cm (4in) mound along the bottom of the trench. Space the crowns 45cm (18in) apart along the centre of the mound, spreading the roots out evenly on either side. (Keep the plants covered until everything is ready; leaving them exposed for any length of time dries out the roots and growth buds and can be fatal.) Cover the crowns with 7.5cm (3in) of soil, then gradually fill in the trench as the shoots grow until it is level with the surrounding soil. Keep weeded and watered, especially in dry weather. Pick off any berries that form; should they germinate, the bed would soon become overcrowded and weeding impossible.

In late autumn when the foliage turns yellow, cut it

down to ground level and apply a thick mulch. For long, white shoots, draw a ridge of soil over the row in spring and apply a general-purpose fertilizer. Level out the ridge the following autumn.

The main pests are slugs and the black-and-orange asparagus beetle. Use slug pellets for the former, malathion for the latter. Violet root rot is an extremely serious fungal disease and infected plants should be dug up and burnt. Do not re-plant with asparagus, or any root vegetable, for three years. Hard frost can turn the shoots black, but if these are cut off new ones will be sent up.

**Harvesting and storing**

Do not pick any shoots for the first two summers after planting as this will severely weaken the young plants. Thereafter, begin picking in late spring and continue until midsummer. Cut 10cm (4in) high shoots 7.5cm (3in) below the soil surface using a long serrated knife or asparagus knife. Allow later shoots to grow undisturbed to provide energy for future crops – and resist the temptation to pick them for flower arranging. Asparagus can be refrigerated for a day or two, or frozen, but these are unworthy treatments for such a marvellous vegetable.

**Varieties**

The most popular foolproof variety is 'Connover's Colossal', with 'Sutton's Favourite' a close second. 'Martha Washington' and 'Mary Washington' are American standbys, and French breeders have recently introduced new varieties – 'Larac' is one – which show great promise.

Asparagus
'Connover's Colossal'

# ASPARAGUS PEAS

The asparagus pea, or winged pea, is botanically neither a pea nor an asparagus, but an unusual, half-hardy annual vetch. Its misleading common names come from the asparagus-like flavour of the young pods, which are shaped like those of peas with four frilly 'wings' along their length. Its sweet-pea-like flowers are dark red.

### Site and soil
Choose a sunny, sheltered spot with light, well-drained soil, enriched with rotted compost the autumn or winter before sowing.

### Cultivation
After the last frost, sow pairs of seeds 5cm (2in) deep and 15cm (6in) apart. If both germinate, remove the weaker seedling; 'doubling up' like this prevents gaping holes in the row should some seeds fail to germinate. Keep well watered and weed free, and when the plants are about 15cm (6in) high, provide pea sticks to help support the floppy, vetch-like growth. Successional sowing extends the cropping period. Any pest and disease problems are likely to be those that afflict peas (see page 136) but the asparagus pea is generally problem-free.

### Harvesting and storing
Pick the young pods from midsummer until the first autumn frosts. The pods should be about 2.5cm (1in) long; any larger and they become tough and stringy. The more pods you pick, the more flowers (and pods) are produced, so check the plants daily. They can be refrigerated for a day or two, but quickly lose their fresh taste and crisp texture.

Asparagus pea

# AUBERGINES

Aubergines, or eggplants, are no longer the curiosity they once were, and can now be found in many greengrocers and supermarkets. Botanically a fruit, the round or club-shaped, shiny purple crop features heavily in Mediterranean and Middle Eastern cuisines. Its bland, very slightly bitter taste is often enlivened by garlic, tomatoes, onions or herbs of the maquis.

Aubergine

### Site and soil
Aubergine is a semi-tropical relative of the tomato, but in cool, temperate climates, it is a very risky crop to grow outdoors. Unless the site is particularly mild and sheltered, the soil rich and free draining, and the summer exceptionally hot, plants outdoors will fail to reach fruition before frost sets in. (If you are determined to have a go, incorporate plenty of well rotted compost into the soil at the base of a south-facing wall during the autumn or winter before planting.)

It is safer to grow aubergines in a greenhouse, either in pots or an open border.

### Cultivation
Sow seed indoors in late winter. Aubergine plants resent root disturbance, so use 7.5cm (3in) pots filled with John Innes potting compost No. 1. Sow three seeds per pot and keep at 16-18°C (60-65°F). Germination can take up to three weeks; once seedlings are big enough to handle,

remove all but the strongest from each pot. Keep watered and, when 15cm (6in) high, pinch out the growing tips to encourage branching and flower formation.

If growing outdoors, harden off the young plants towards the end of spring and plant out after the last frost, 75cm (30in) apart. Stake to support the heavy growth, which can be up to 1m (3ft) high.

If growing under glass, once roots fill the pot, move to a 15cm (6in) pot filled with John Innes No. 3. Ultimately, the plants will need 22.5cm (9in) pots. Alternatively, plant into the open greenhouse border and stake as above.

Allow only four fruit to form and pinch out subsequent flowers. Once the fruit starts swelling, feed with a proprietary tomato fertilizer once a week.

Aubergines enjoy heat, but the hotter and drier the conditions, the more troublesome red spider mite can be. Mist the plants daily, particularly the leaf undersides, and never let the compost or soil dry out. If an infestation does occur, treat with derris.

Watering also helps the fruit to set, but be careful of over-watering which can encourage grey mould, or botrytis. If this happens, remove and burn the infected parts, increase ventilation and raise the temperature if possible.

**Harvesting and storing**
Harvest aubergines when they have stopped growing but still have shiny, well-coloured

Aubergine
'Long Purple'

Aubergine
'Easter Egg'

skins. Aubergines with dull skins are over-ripe; the flesh will be bitter and filled with seeds. Optimum size depends on the cultivar grown. Time of harvest depends on growing conditions, but is usually from midsummer to mid-autumn.

Aubergines can be refrigerated for up to a week, but since a glut of aubergines is unlikely they are best picked just before cooking.

**Varieties**
'Long Purple' is the traditional favourite; newer varieties include the $F_1$ hybrids 'Moneymaker' and 'Dusky'. Most unusual is 'Easter Egg', which carries a dozen or more fruit, the size, shape and colour of a hen's egg.

# BEANS, BROAD

Broad beans

Broad beans are beginner's beans, and one of the first vegetable crops of summer, when people have had more than their fill of winter brassicas. Broad beans, with their tough constitution, are easy to grow, and the only beans hardy enough to be sown in autumn. Unfortunately, they also have a reputation for being tough in the kitchen, which, though sometimes true, is not their fault. Commercially grown broad beans are harvested when they are at their biggest — for obvious reasons — by which time the beans are tough-skinned and flavourless. Also, several days may elapse between harvesting and sale. Young, freshly picked beans are quite another matter, and worth growing if you have the space. When very young, they can be cooked like French beans, or served in the Italian manner with salami and sheep's cheese as an antipasto.

### Site and soil
Broad beans prefer rich, deep, not-too-acid soil that is heavy but not waterlogged. For autumn sowing, shelter and mild weather are essential.

Broad beans should follow a crop for which the soil has been enriched with well rotted garden compost. No additional organic matter is necessary, though the soil should be dug over before sowing and a general-purpose fertilizer raked in.

Broad bean
'Aquadulce'

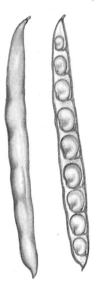

Broad bean
'Imperial Green'

Alternatively, dig organic matter into the soil the autumn or winter before a spring sowing, and rake in a general-purpose fertilizer as above. Remember not to follow one bean crop with another as this encourages disease.

Though there are dwarf-growing varieties, most broad beans grow 1-1.2m (3-4ft) high, so anything growing behind them will be shaded. (Summer crops of lettuce and spinach would appreciate such shade and be less likely to bolt as a result.) The tall, bushy plants also act as a wind break, provided they are well staked.

## Cultivation
Autumn sowing has benefits, but also carries the risk that young plants may be killed in a severe winter. On the other hand, if they do survive, cropping will be earlier and the plants themselves less vulnerable to blackfly. Also, a failed autumn sowing can be replaced by a spring one. Some varieties are hardier than others and longpods are usually preferred for autumn sowing. Sow in mid- to late autumn; earlier sowings will result in lush growth which will almost certainly be killed.

'Spring' sowing can actually begin in late winter, provided the ground isn't frozen solid or a quagmire. Successional sowings can continue until late spring, which should give crops through late summer. Cloching earlier sowings is beneficial.

Sow seed 15cm (6in) apart and 5cm (2in) deep, in double rows spaced 15cm (6in) apart.

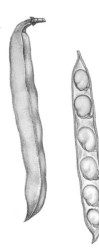

Broad bean
'Green Windsor'

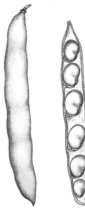

Broad bean
'White Windsor'

If sowing several double rows, space each pair 60cm (2ft) apart.

Broad beans can be sown under glass in midwinter, then hardened off and planted out in early spring. One old-fashioned method consisted of pushing four seeds, evenly spaced apart, into an upside-down piece of turf. When the seeds germinated, the turf was cut into four and each of the seedlings planted out in its small square.

The modern-day equivalent is the peat pot; alternatively, sow seeds, spaced 5cm (2in) apart, in seed trays. Keep seedlings started under glass as cool and well ventilated as possible; warm, close conditions are fatal.

Whether sown indoors or out, germination is bound to be less than one hundred percent, and a few extra should be sown to act as replacements.

Young plants are vulnerable to competition from weeds, so hoe regularly, and hand weed when necessary. Broad beans don't climb and, except for dwarf varieties, do need support. Their root systems are relatively small and shallow compared to their tall, leafy top growth. Earthing up the soil round the base of the young plants does help stabilize them, but stout stakes and two or three rows of wire or strong twine prevent the plants from blowing over. No feeding is necessary and, except in very dry weather, young plants won't need watering.

Pinch out the growing tips when the first pods appear, to encourage their development and discourage blackfly, which are fond of the succulent shoots. (See French Beans, page 54, and Runner Beans, page 59, for other problems.) Once pods start to swell, ensure a regular supply of water.

## Harvesting and storing

Young beans, up to 7.5cm (3in) long, can be picked and eaten whole like French beans. For shelling, pick the pods when you can feel and see the bulge of the beans inside. Open one pod; if the beans are too small, wait a few days and try again. Beans in their pods will keep for several days in a refrigerator, or they can be shelled and frozen for several months.

## Varieties

Broad beans can be green- or white-seeded, and longpod, Windsor or dwarf varieties. Longpods are the hardiest and produce the biggest yields. Favourites include 'Imperial Green', 'Imperial White' and the white-seeded 'Aquadulce'. Windsors are less hardy, with smaller yields, but have a sweeter flavour. 'Green Windsor' and 'White Windsor' are traditional choices, though improved strains have been developed. 'The Sutton' and 'Bonny Lad' are both white-seeded dwarf forms.

# BEANS, FRENCH

Climbing French beans

French beans are typical of so many half-hardy vegetables grown in temperate climates: their lives are governed by the timing of the last spring frost and the first autumn one. Still, they are pretty plants, with an undemanding nature and a very high yield for the amount of space they take up. French beans can also be grown in large pots by gardeners with only a balcony or concrete patio.

**Site and soil**
Never follow one bean with another in crop rotation. Choose a spot that is sunny and sheltered (particularly for climbing varieties) with free-draining, not-too-acid soil. Dig well rotted compost into the soil the autumn before sowing or planting, and if necessary apply lime in midwinter. A week before sowing or planting, rake in a general-purpose fertilizer.

**Cultivation**
In the days of generously heated greenhouses, French beans could be grown all year round. Today, the crop is more realistically approached as one to be started in mid-spring, under glass with a little artificial heat, or outdoors under cloches.

To avoid root disturbance if sowing indoors, sow in pairs in peat pots, then remove the weaker seedling. Just enough heat to keep the frost off should suffice; too much heat results

Dwarf French beans

in lush, vulnerable growth.

To sow outdoors, make drills 5cm (2in) deep, in double rows 30cm (12in) apart. If more than one double row is planted, leave space between for easy access.

It is a good idea to put the cloches in position a week or two before sowing to warm up the soil. Sow the beans 15cm (6in) apart, with a few extra sown at the end of the row to cover for the inevitable germination failures. Cover with soil then tread firm. Both mice and birds are fond of bean seeds, so never leave seeds exposed on the soil surface; they can be given additional protection by netting and black cotton. Scatter slug pellets as well.

Open sowing, without the protection of cloches, can commence in late spring. Plants started out under glass can be hardened off then and planted out as above. To get an extended period of cropping until the first frost, sow successionally through early summer.

Never allow the beans to go dry at the roots; water as often as the weather demands. Hoeing between rows and hand weeding between plants is essential while the plants are small; later, their dense foliage will suppress competition. Hoeing also keeps the soil surface broken up, allowing water to penetrate to the roots beneath.

Dwarf French beans are said not to need support, but pea sticks help keep the heavy crops from dragging on the ground.

French bean
'The Prince'

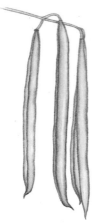

French bean
'Blue Lake'

Climbing French beans need support on a larger scale (see Runner Beans, page 56).

In early summer, mulch with leaf mould, straw or well rotted compost to help conserve soil moisture. In early autumn the non-climbing varieties can be protected with high 'barn' cloches for late cropping. When all cropping is finished, cut the plants off at ground level, leaving the roots in the ground to increase the soil's nitrogen content.

Beans can be beset with many troubles (see Broad Beans, page 51, and Runner Beans, page 59), but good cultivation minimizes problems. The best precaution against bean beetle and halo blight is to buy seeds from a reliable source. When sowing, destroy any seeds which have small, round holes (a sign of bean-beetle infestation) or those with wrinkled, pale spotted or blistered skins (a sign of halo blight).

For container growing, use well-crocked pots, 22.5cm (9in) or more in diameter, and John Innes potting compost No. 3. Water copiously as compost dries out quickly.

**Harvesting and storing**
Begin picking pods for eating whole (*haricots verts*) when they are about 10cm (4in) long. Inspect the plants daily; the more pods are picked, the more are produced. Never pull pods from the plant; use scissors, secateurs or a pinching action of the thumb and forefinger.

The beans inside should not bulge through the pod, and the

French bean
'Kinghorn Wax'

latter should snap if bent (hence the name snap beans). *Haricots verts* are most delicious eaten immediately after picking, but can be refrigerated or blanched and frozen.

To harvest semi-ripe beans (*flageolets*) for drying, pick when the beans are fully swollen and the pods beginning to change colour. For fully ripe beans, or *haricots*, wait until the pods are pale brown and starting to split. In both cases, shell the beans and lay them out in a single layer until bone dry, then store in an airtight jar.

## Varieties

Most popular are the green-podded, dwarf-growing sorts, such as 'The Prince', 'Masterpiece' and 'Tendergreen'. Climbing green beans include 'Blue Lake' (suitable for drying as well) and 'Garrafal Oro'. For drying as *haricots*, 'Chevrier Vert' is the best bean. Purple-podded varieties include the dwarf-growing 'Royal Burgundy' and 'Purple Podded Climbing'. The pods, however, turn green when cooked. Yellow-podded beans, such as 'Kinghorn Wax' and 'Mont d'Or', retain their colour and exquisite flavour when cooked. There are varieties suitable for early sowing, sandy soil and cold conditions; check with your seed merchant.

French bean
'Royal Burgundy'

# BEANS, RUNNER

Climbing runner beans

No allotment or vegetable garden is complete without its rows or wigwams of runner beans, with their ornamental foliage, scarlet, bicoloured or white flowers and prolific crops. Likewise, no summer is complete without a go at the 'bean machine', manually or electrically slicing the long, flat pods into thin diagonal strips.

The runner bean is a South American perennial grown as a half-hardy annual. It crops from midsummer to the first frost, and a glut of runner beans is usually the rule not the exception.

**Site and soil**
Choose a sunny, sheltered site and a rich, deep, well-drained soil. (Thin, sandy soils and cold clays are unsuitable.) Dwarf runner beans excepted, the plants grow to a height of 1.8m (6ft), and present a dense, leafy wall to the wind. A whole row, if not adequately supported, can collapse in the face of a summer gale. On the other hand, a strong row of runner beans acts as a wind break itself, sheltering nearby crops. Runner beans also shade nearby plants, and for this reason are often planted as the end row or near a wall. Alternatively, use the shade for summer lettuce or spinach.

Runner beans can follow onions, brassicas or potatoes in crop rotation. These beans are greedy feeders and well rotted compost should be dug into the soil in the autumn before sowing or planting. Too much nitrogen, however, in the soil can result in lush foliage, with the flowers failing to 'set' and poor crops. Applying sulphate of potash, 50g per sq m (2oz per sq yd), before planting or sowing helps balance any excess of nitrogen.

Runner beans dislike very acid soil; if necessary, work lime into the soil in midwinter.

**Cultivation**

Though old-fashioned gardeners sometimes lifted and stored the tuberous roots of runner beans, like lifting and storing dahlias, from one year to the next, plants today are grown annually from seed. Young plants can be bought from a garden centre. Alternatively, seeds can be sown under glass in mid-spring for planting out after the last frost, or sown outdoors in late spring (mid-spring if cloches are used).

Buying plants or starting seeds under glass buys time, a precious commodity in cold districts or unusually late springs. To avoid root disturbance, sow seeds in peat pots, providing cool but frost-free conditions. Never force germination as weak plants result. Whether sowing indoors or out, sow more than you need because a few seeds inevitably fail to germinate. And when planting young runner beans outdoors, make sure they are fully hardened off; the fact that trays are sitting outdoors in a garden centre is no guarantee of this.

There are several methods of supporting runner beans. If

Runner bean
'Enorma'

only a few plants are grown, make a circle about 2.1m (7ft) in diameter using seven or eight bean poles, tied together at the top to form a wigwam. Train one plant up each pole. A smaller tripod of poles will support three plants, grown in a tiny garden or an ornamental border.

For long rows, use bean poles, either singly or in pairs, or netting. Single canes should be inserted 30cm (12in) vertically into the soil, with at least 1.8m (6ft) of pole above ground. Space the poles 30cm (12in) apart, and place a stout supporting post at either end of the row. Run a strong wire from post to post, attaching each pole to it along the top, and fix struts or guy wires to the end posts for added stability.

If used in pairs, the poles should be spaced 45cm (18in) apart, with 30cm (12in) between pairs in the row. Angle the poles so each pair crosses at the top, then fix a series of overlapping horizontal poles in the crotches of the crossed poles.

Lastly, large-mesh plastic netting fixed to stout end pieces can be used. Intermediate posts, every 1.8m (6ft) or so, are necessary to help take the weight and all posts should have struts.

Sow seeds (or plant seedlings) so that each plant ultimately has a pole for support; if using mesh, space plants 30cm (12in) apart. Place a few slug pellets near the rows and cover with cloches in the case of early sowings.

Young plants need help in starting to climb. They can be

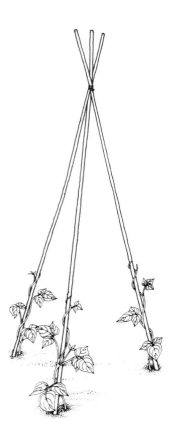

A wigwam to support runner beans

loosely tied to the bottom of poles or netting; eventually, the plants will climb and cling of their own accord. (Tightly twisting twine round bamboo canes or poles, from top to bottom, gives something for the plants to grip.)

Keep young plants weeded and the surrounding soil surface loose. Water thoroughly in dry weather and, if possible, mulch the damp soil in early summer with leaf mould, well rotted garden compost or straw. Liquid feeds from time to time, once the plants have started flowering, extend the period of cropping. Pinch out the growing points once the top of the support system is reached.

As with all legumes, leave the roots in the soil once harvesting is finished to increase its nitrogen content.

As well as those troubles mentioned in Broad Beans (page 51) and French Beans (page 54) runner beans can suffer from anthracnose, a disease encouraged by damp, cold conditions. Symptoms are sunken brown patches on leaves, stems and pods. A reliable seed source is the best precaution. Burn infected plants and spray the remainder with a half-strength Bordeaux mixture.

**Harvesting and storing**
Don't be mesmerized by giantism in runner beans; large pods are tough, stringy and tasteless. Begin picking pods 15cm (6in) long, before the seeds begin to bulge. Pick regularly, because any pods allowed to mature fully inhibit

Runner bean
'Hammond's Dwarf Scarlet'

the production of further pods.

Runner beans keep for up to a week if refrigerated, although freezing is the only real solution for large quantities.

## Varieties

Climbing runner beans of proven reputation include 'Achievement', 'Mergoles' and 'Enorma'; 'Sunset', 'Scarlet Emperor' and 'Kelvedon Marvel'. The last three can also be grown as bush, or ground,

beans. The growing tips are pinched out when 30cm (12in) high, and subsequent side shoots are pinched out weekly. Bushy plants result, needing only twiggy pea sticks for support, but crops are smaller than those from plants allowed to grow normally. There are also genuine dwarf runner beans, which reach a height of 45cm (18in); 'Hammond's Dwarf Scarlet' is the most popular.

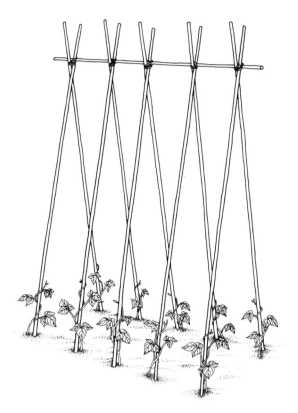

Poles to support runner beans

# BEETROOT

Beetroot.
'Torono'

Beetroot
'Cheltenham
Green Top'

Pickled beetroot is the bane of school lunches and huge, woody beetroots are equally unloved in the kitchen. There is another side to beetroot: young, freshly picked and cooked roots have a deliciously sweet taste and tender texture. Also, young beetroot leaves, and the mature leaves of yellow and white varieties, can be cooked like spinach. It is an easy crop to grow and gives a sense of pride and self-sufficiency to the gardener in return for very little effort.

**Site and soil**
In a traditional crop rotation, beetroot often follows French or runner beans, peas or celery. Deep, sandy soil is best, particularly for long varieties of beetroot. Very acid soil is unsuitable; if necessary, work in lime in midwinter. Work in well rotted compost the autumn before sowing. (Freshly enriched soil results in forked, useless roots.) Finally, a week before sowing, rake in a general-purpose fertilizer.

**Cultivation**
The trickiest part of growing beetroot is getting the timing right, and sowing little and often is the key. Start sowing globe varieties for harvesting young in early spring, if the weather is mild and the garden sheltered or if you can offer cloche protection. Continue at two-week intervals until midsummer for crops from

Beetroot
'Boltardy'

Beetroot
'Burpee's Golden'

early summer through autumn.
Sow beetroot for winter storage
– whether globe, cylindrical or
long – in late spring or early
summer. Earlier sowings for
winter storage would result in
over-large tough roots.

Though breeders have
developed monogerm seeds,
which produce only one
seedling per seed capsule,
normally each beetroot 'seed'
contains several seeds, each
capable of germination. Soak
the capsules in water for a few
hours before sowing to hasten
germination. Sow the capsules
5cm (2in) apart, in drills 2.5cm
(1in) deep and 30cm (12in)
apart. Cover and firm the
surface and protect from birds
with netting or pea guards
(half-cylinders of small-mesh
wire netting, available
commercially).

Thin the seedlings as soon as
they are large enough to
handle, retaining only the
strongest at each station. Thin
again when the leaves are 5cm
(2in) tall, leaving 10cm (4in)
between globe varieties, and
slightly more for intermediate
and long types.

Keep the plants weed free; it
is just possible to hoe between
rows, but hand weeding
between plants is also
necessary. Provide a steady,
even supply of water to prevent
stunted poor crops and split
roots, which result from too
little water followed by too
much.

Mangold fly may cause
blistered and browned leaves;
pick off and burn any leaves
showing signs of infestation
and spray the crop with
malathion. Bolting is usually

caused by dry or poor soil, or crowded growing conditions.

**Harvesting and storing**

Roots 2.5cm (1in) in diameter are useful in the kitchen; harvest alternate plants, leaving the others to grow on. Continue picking as needed, and in mid-autumn harvest roots grown for winter storage. Don't let the roots grow larger than 8cm (3½in) across or they will be woody and tasteless.

Use a spade or fork to loosen the roots, being careful not to pierce them. Twist off the foliage, leaving about 5cm (2in) of stem attached to the root. Clean off any soil adhering to the root, check that it is not damaged or diseased, then store in layers in a box topped up with sand or peat. Keep in a cold but frost-free place. Beets will keep for two weeks or more refrigerated but do not freeze well.

**Varieties**

Globe, or round, varieties are the most popular for quick growing and harvesting young. For early sowing choose a bolt-resistant type, such as 'Boltardy' or 'Avonearly'. Maincrop varieties include 'Detroit', 'Globe', the yellow-fleshed 'Burpee's Golden' and the white-fleshed 'Snowhite'.

Cylindrical, or intermediate varieties are usually grown for winter storage; 'Forono' and 'Cylindra' are the most popular intermediates. Long beetroot is really too big for normal kitchen use and is usually grown for exhibition; 'Cheltenham Green Top' is a favourite.

Beetroot
'Snowhite'

# BROCCOLI

Broccoli is the home grower's first introduction to brassicas in any alphabetically arranged gardening book. In a way, this is a pity because although broccoli is a popular vegetable, its botanical nomenclature is very confusing. The bright-green, large broccoli spears, often sold as a frozen vegetable, are actually calabrese, a perennial grown as a half-hardy annual. Purple and white forms of sprouting broccoli produce many tiny curds at the ends of small stalks and are grown as hardy biennials. To add to the confusion, there is a hardy perennial broccoli and one which resembles cauliflower (see Cauliflowers, page 80).

## Site and soil

Never follow one brassica with another in crop rotation. Choose a sunny site with rich, well drained, neutral or alkaline soil. If the soil has not been enriched for a previous crop, work in well rotted compost in the autumn before planting. Lime, if necessary, in midwinter and rake in a general-purpose fertilizer a week before planting.

Calabrese is a short-lived plant, sown in spring and harvested before the first frost, but sprouting broccoli remains in the garden for up to a year, and perennial broccoli for several years. Site the latter out of the way of quick-growing crops, perhaps in a corner.

Broccoli
White-sprouting

Broccoli
Purple-sprouting

## Cultivation

Sow outdoors in a seed bed in mid- or late spring. Make the drills 15mm (½in) deep and 15cm (6in) apart. Once seedlings appear, usually within two weeks of sowing, thin to 7.5cm (3in) apart. When they are about 7.5cm (3in) high, they are ready for transplanting. Thoroughly water the seedlings the day before transplanting; when lifting them, try to retain as much soil as possible around the roots. Using a dibber, make holes 10cm (4in) deep and 50cm (2ft) apart for sprouting broccoli, 45cm (18in) apart for calabrese. Insert the plants so they are buried deeper in the soil than they were in the seed bed; this encourages root formation and increases stability against wind. Firm the soil round the plant, then check by pulling at a leaf – if the plant comes up, start again. Water well, and keep watered whenever the soil is dry.

Hoe or hand weed to keep weed competition down, and mulch in late spring or early summer with well rotted compost, leaf mould or straw. In autumn, earth up the soil round the lower stems of sprouting broccoli and, on very exposed and windy sites, stake each plant. Check that plants have not been lifted by hard frost, and re-firm as necessary.

Many pests and diseases afflict brassicas (see also Brussels Sprouts, page 68, Cabbages, page 72, Cauliflowers, page 81, Kale page 106). Birds, especially sparrows and pigeons are fond of stripping the leaves; netting

Broccoli
Calabrese

Broccoli
'Nine Star Perennial'

young seedlings and grown plants in winter is the best precaution. The caterpillars of cabbage white butterflies and moths make irregular holes in the leaves; hand pick small infestations and spray severe ones with fenetrothion.

**Harvesting and storing**
Pick calabrese from late summer until the first frost; sprouting broccoli from early winter to late spring, depending on variety; and perennial broccoli in early and mid-spring. Pick before flower buds open; once they open, taste and texture deteriorate and future production of buds is inhibited. Cut off any central heads first; this encourages the production of smaller, secondary sprouts, which can be cut when 10cm (4in) long. When harvesting is finished, dig up and burn the stalks as they are too tough to decompose as compost.

**Varieties**
'Nine Star Perennial' is the only perennial variety; to keep it cropping over several years, never let any buds flower on the plant. 'Early White Sprouting' and 'Late White Sprouting' are self-explanatory varieties of white-sprouting broccoli. 'Christmas Purple Sprouting' is the earliest of the purple-sprouting broccolis, followed by 'Early Purple Sprouting' and 'Late Purple Sprouting'. Quick growing $F_1$ hybrid calabreses include 'Express Corona' and 'Green Comet'. 'Corvet' is slower growing, but is a particularly heavy cropper.

# BRUSSELS SPROUTS

Brussels sprouts

Overcooked sprouts, like overcooked cabbage, are the epitome of bad food. Young, tender sprouts, lightly cooked, are another matter altogether, and while little claim can be made for the superiority of home-grown sprouts over shop-bought ones, there is something satisfying about a perfectly hardy crop that can be harvested, depending on variety, from early summer through to the following early spring.

## Site and soil

An open, sunny, sheltered site and firm, neutral or alkaline soil are best. It should be free-draining and rich, but not too rich; if the ground was not enriched for a previous crop, work in well rotted compost in the autumn before planting. Lime the soil in midwinter if necessary, and rake in a general-purpose fertilizer a week before planting. Never follow one brassica with another.

Some varieties grow quite tall and can shade nearby crops; the taller they are, the more important shelter from the prevailing wind becomes.

## Cultivation

Sow outdoors in a seed bed from late winter to mid-spring. Make the drills 15mm (½in) deep and 15cm (6in) apart. Sow thinly, cover with soil, then firm. Alternatively, sow in seed trays kept in a sunny and cool but frost-free spot. As

Brussels sprouts
'Citadel'

soon as the seedlings are large enough to handle – germination is usually within two weeks – thin or prick out to 7.5cm (3in) apart.

Transplant, after the last frost, to their final position, spacing the plants 60-75cm (2-2½ft) apart. Water the seed bed the day before transplanting and, as with broccoli, place the seedlings lower in the ground than they were in the seed bed. Firm the soil after planting; loose planting results in poor crops. Water thoroughly and water again whenever the weather is dry. Mulch in late spring or early summer and stake the plants in autumn. Earthing up around shallow roots affords additional stability and frost protection.

Like all brassicas, Brussels sprouts are vulnerable to club root, a serious fungal disease. Infected plants are stunted, with leaves that are blue-tinged and wilted. Dig up any suspicious plants and inspect the roots; if they are swollen, smelly and discoloured, the plant is infected and must be destroyed. Very acid and poorly drained soils are associated with club root; correcting these problems is the best preventative. Dipping the roots in calomel or benomyl before transplanting also helps. (See also Broccoli, page 65, Cabbages, page 72, Cauliflowers, page 81, Kale, page 106).

Blown sprouts, which never form a hard heart, are due to infertile soil, overcrowded or loose planting or insufficient water in dry weather. $F_1$

varieties tend to be less vulnerable to these conditions.

## Harvesting and storing

With this crop, small is beautiful. Once the lower leaves start to yellow, remove them and begin harvesting the crop from the bottom of the stalk up. The sprouts should be tightly closed and 20-25cm ($\frac{3}{4}$-1in) in diameter. Remove them by hand or with a knife. Unless harvesting $F_1$ hybrids all at once for freezing, only pick a few sprouts at a time from any one plant, and always remove over-ripe, blown sprouts missed from earlier pickings. At the end of the season cut off the green tops and cook as spring greens, then dig up and burn the stalks.

Sprouts can be refrigerated for up to a week, or frozen.

## Varieties

$F_1$ hybrids tend to be more compact than old-fashioned varieties and their sprouts mature all at once, although they do remain closed for some weeks. The earliest $F_1$ hybrid is 'Peer Gynt', followed by the mid-season 'Citadel' and 'Perfect Line', and the late-cropping 'Rampart'. Old-fashioned sprouts tend to be larger plants, with sprouts forming over a longer period. Noteworthy varieties include 'Noisette', whose small sprouts have a nutty flavour, and the red-sprouted 'Rubine'.

# CABBAGES

Cabbage
'Durham Early'

Cabbage
'Hispi'

The cabbage family is a sprawling one and rather hard to divide into neat categories. Plant breeders have had a field day with this crop and there are dozens of varieties, each suited to quite specific conditions and timing. To simplify matters, spring cabbages – conical-shaped spring greens – are sown the previous summer. Cabbages for harvesting in autumn, winter or summer are sown the previous late winter to late spring. In addition to green cabbages, there are white and red cabbages, crinkly-leaved Savoys and Chinese cabbages (see page 74). As well as conical cabbages, there are round and drumhead (flat-topped round) ones.

Cabbage could never be considered a delicacy and in a small garden growing summer cabbage is probably a waste of space; tomatoes, beans, peas and lettuce are more seasonal and appropriate. Nonetheless, cabbage is generally an extremely hardy and long-suffering crop, providing greens for the kitchen long after more fickle and ephemeral crops have disappeared, and long before they reappear.

**Site and soil**
Never follow a brassica crop with cabbage. Choose a sunny spot with neutral or alkaline, rich but not recently manured, free-draining soil. If necessary, work in well rotted compost in the autumn and lime in

midwinter; firm soil is essential and any preparation should be done well before planting. A week before planting, apply a general-purpose fertilizer.

**Cultivation**

Whatever the timing, cabbages are sown successively in seed beds and the seedlings transplanted to their permanent position when about 10cm (4in) high. Sow thinly in drills 15mm (½in) deep and 15cm (6in) apart. Early sowings of summer cabbage, in late winter or early spring, are best done with the aid of cloches to warm up the soil and keep off the worst of the weather. The seed bed can be very dry in midsummer when spring cabbage is sown. Water before sowing, if necessary.

As soon as the seedlings are large enough to handle, thin them to 7.5cm (3in) apart. The day before transplanting, water the seedlings thoroughly. Final spacing depends on variety. Space spring cabbage 10-15cm (4-6in) apart in rows 30cm (12in) apart. Space compact summer, autumn and winter cabbage 30cm (12in) apart; larger-growing varieties 45-60cm (18-24in) apart, in rows similarly spaced apart.

Lift the seedlings with as much soil attached to the roots as possible, then plant as quickly and firmly as possible. so the roots don't dry out. Check for firmness by tugging at a leaf, then water thoroughly. Protect from birds by netting the rows.

Hoe and hand weed as necessary; hoeing also helps keep the soil surface from

Cabbage
'January King'

Cabbage
'Celtic'

Cabbage
'Red Drumhead'

Cabbage
'Savoy King'

becoming hard and impenetrable. Water in dry weather. When the leaves touch, remove every other spring cabbage; these thinnings can go straight to the kitchen.

Feed autumn, winter and summer cabbages during the growing period with applications of diluted liquid fertilizer. Do not feed spring cabbages; the lush growth that would result is vulnerable to winter weather. (After a bad winter, though, they would benefit from a nitrogenous fertilizer in late winter and early spring.)

Before the first frost, earth up the stems of late autumn, winter and spring cabbages to provide stability and frost protection. After heavy frost, check whether any have been lifted and re-firm if they are loose.

Cabbages are affected by many pests, of which cabbage root fly and flea beetle are particularly annoying. The former are most active in spring and early summer, when eggs hatch and maggots eat their way through the stem and into the roots. Above-ground symptoms include blue-tinged, wilted leaves and stunted or dead plants. There is no cure; sprinkling bromophos or diazinon around newly transplanted seedlings is a good preventative measure. Small round holes in the leaves of young plants, particularly in spring, are a sign that flea beetle is present. Spray with an insecticide suitable for crops; as a preventive, dust young plants with derris.

For a more complete rogues' gallery of brassica problems, see Broccoli (page 65), Brussels Sprouts (page 68), Cauliflowers (page 81) and Kale (page 106).

## Harvesting and storing

Begin harvesting when the hearts are firm. Either dig them up, roots and all, or cut the heads off just above the lowest leaves using a sharp knife. Make a small cross in the top of the remaining stump of spring or summer crops to stimulate the growth of fresh greens for cutting. When these are harvested, dig up and burn the stalks.

Cabbage can be refrigerated for a week or more. Cabbage can also be frozen, though it seems a waste of freezer space, particularly as autumn cabbages with firm hearts will keep for several months in a cool, frost-free shed. Pickling red cabbage is a traditional method of storage.

## Varieties

Winter cabbages include the early 'Christmas Drumhead'; the $F_1$ hybrids 'Jupiter' and 'Celtic'; and the white 'Holland Late Winter'. Spring cabbages include the compact-growing 'April' and 'Offenham Spring Bounty'; and the old-fashioned 'Wheeler's Imperial'. Summer and autumn cabbages are generally lumped together in seed catalogues. These include the round, compact 'Primo' ('Golden Acre'); the conical $F_1$ hybrid 'Hispi' and 'Greyhound'; and the compact $F_1$ hybrid 'Minicole'. Red cabbages fall into the summer and autumn category; 'Red Drumhead' ('Niggy') with a compact, deep purple head is the one usually grown. Savoys, according to variety, span the seasons from late summer through early spring, from mid- or late spring sowings. 'Best of All' is early, followed by 'January King' and 'Ormskirk Late'.

# CABBAGES, CHINESE

Chinese cabbage is a relatively recent addition to the brassica scene. Its taste is more subtle than that of cabbage and, unlike other brassicas, it is very quick growing. It can be served raw in autumn salad and steamed in Chinese dishes; or the midribs of the outer leaves can be cooked like asparagus.

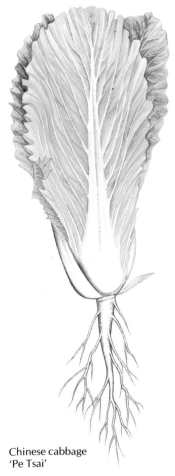

Chinese cabbage
'Pe Tsai'

### Site and soil
Neutral or alkaline, reasonably fertile, firm soil, and sun or light shade are suitable. (See Brussels Sprouts, page 67, for details.)

### Cultivation
Chinese cabbage resents being transplanted. Sow seed individually, 10cm (4in) apart, in drills 15mm (½in) deep and 30cm (12in) apart. Sow early varieties successionally in mid- or late spring; the remainder successionally in midsummer. Thin seedlings to 30cm (12in) apart and keep weed-free. Regular watering is essential if the plants are not to bolt; a mulch around the young plants helps the soil retain its moisture and keeps weeds down. When the heads start to swell, tie them loosely to blanch the inner leaves. Slugs can be troublesome.

### Harvesting and storing
Harvest from late summer to late autumn, depending on variety and weather. When maximum size is reached, harvest as soon as possible. Over-mature plants tend to go to seed, and Chinese cabbage keeps for up to two weeks refrigerated. Cloche end-of-season crops to protect from frost and wet.

### Varieties
The $F_1$ hybrid 'Sampan' is an early, bolt-resistant variety. Later varieties include 'Tip Top' and 'Pe Tsai'.

# CARDOONS

Cardoon is an obscure vegetable like the globe artichoke in appearance but grown for its blanched stalks, which are boiled in chunks, rather than its flower heads. It is a huge perennial, grown as an annual, and more suited to flower borders than tiny vegetable plots. Its curiosity value is high; its culinary value lower.

### Site and soil
Choose rich, well drained soil and a sunny, sheltered site, where the shade cardoon casts won't be a nuisance. In early spring, dig a trench 30cm (12in) wide and deep and fork in well rotted compost.

### Cultivation
In mid-spring, sow groups of three seeds spaced 60cm (2ft) apart along the trench. Remove all but the strongest seedling from each group when they are large enough to handle. Keep weeds down and water well, flooding the trenches from time to time. In late summer, begin blanching by removing any wilted or damaged leaves, then wrapping the remaining leaves tightly with black polythene tied with string. Partially fill in the trench with the excavated soil, and continue until the process is complete in early autumn.

Cardoon

### Harvesting and storing
Six weeks after blanching, begin harvesting. Dig up the plant, cut off its roots and discard the outer leaves. As harvesting can take place over several weeks and crops are small, storage is not a problem.

## CARROTS

Unless you have a good-sized garden there is little point in growing huge carrots for winter storage. Those in the shops are inexpensive and taste much the same as carrots stored from a home-grown crop. Small, quick-growing carrots, though, are quite another matter, worth accommodating in even the tiniest garden for the beauty of their delicate, fern-like foliage as well as for the fresh flavour and crisp texture of the roots.

**Site and soil**
The ideal soil is sandy, free draining, deep and fertile, but not overly rich. Old-fashioned, long-rooted carrots need these conditions, but most people grow short-rooted or intermediate (medium-sized) carrots which crop well in other soils. Even for the most tolerant, short-rooted types stony, recently enriched or water-logged soils are unsuitable.

Dig over the soil in autumn, then, a week before sowing, make the seed bed and rake in a general-purpose fertilizer. If carrot fly maggots have been a problem previously, killing seedlings and tunnelling through roots, rake in bromophos as well.

Early crops need full sun; maincrops benefit from a bit of light shade. In traditional crop rotation carrots often follow peas, beans or onions.

**Cultivation**
Always follow the suggested sowing times on seed packets

Carrot
'New Red Intermediate'

Carrot
'Amerstam Forcing'

Carrot
'Early French Frame'

and choose varieties suitable for your cropping schedule. Begin the first sowings of short-rooted types in early spring, under cloches or cold frames, for harvesting in early summer. From mid-spring onwards sow short-rooted and intermediate types, little and often, in the open ground, for harvesting from midsummer onwards. Make a last sowing of short-rooted carrots in late summer for picking in late autumn; provide cloche protection for the last few weeks. For maincrops, sow intermediate or long-rooted types, in mid- or late spring or early summer, for lifting and storing in autumn.

More than for most other vegetables, thin sowing is essential. Not only do the young roots resent the disturbance and loosened soil caused by thinning, but the dreaded carrot fly is attracted to the smell of the leaves, and handling them during thinning releases the scent. Old-fashioned methods of ensuring thin sowing include mixing the seed with sand or with radish seed. The latter germinates quickly – carrots can take two weeks or more and provides a quick catch crop as well as marking the rows. Sowing rows of chives or parsley near carrots is the traditional way of masking the smell of carrot foliage.

Sow the seed in drills 15mm (½in) deep and15cm (6in) apart for quick-growing carrots, 30cm (12in) apart for maincrops. (In dry weather water thoroughly the day before sowing.) Cover with soil and firm.

As soon as the seedlings are large enough to handle, thin in stages, first to 15mm (½in) apart, then 2.5cm (1in) and ultimately 5cm (2in) for quick-growing crops, and twice that for maincrops. Later thinnings can be used in the kitchen. To discourage carrot fly, thin in the evening having watered the ground thoroughly first. Firm the soil after every thinning and never leave thinnings lying around.

Hoe between rows, hand weed between plants and, again, re-firm the soil afterwards. Water in dry weather to prevent the roots splitting when it does eventually rain, also as a further preventive for carrot fly and aphids. The latter attack the foliage in dry weather and cause stunting; hand pick and destroy infested leaves, then spray the remainder with fenitrothion. Earth up any roots that start to grow out of the soil to keep them from turning green.

In the days when manure was freely available, very early crops of short-rooted carrots were sown from midwinter onwards. A layer of fermenting manure, mixed with straw and leafmould, was topped with fine soil and then a cold frame. The heat given off by the fermenting material, combined with the solar gain of the cold frame, was sufficient to germinate the seed; if you have the necessary ingredients, you may wish to try this method.

**Harvesting and storing**
Early, quick-growing crops can be harvested as and when

Carrot
'Chantenay Red Cored'

needed. (Later thinnings are a form of harvest.) Use a fork to loosen the soil, then pull out the roots by their foliage. Theoretically, maincrops can be overwintered in the ground in mild gardens, but they are usually lifted in mid-autumn and stored, not touching one another, in boxes of sand or peat.

Harvest on a dry day and remove any soil clinging to the roots. Split or otherwise damaged roots should be eaten immediately, not stored, if the self-descriptive black rot or woolly white sclerotina rot is not to ruin the entire crop. Check stored roots regularly for any sign of fungal infection. Carrots can be refrigerated for weeks or blanched and frozen, the latter treatment better reserved for tiny carrots.

## Varieties

Short-rooted carrots include the round 'Early French Frame' and ultra-tolerant 'Kundulus'. The earliest finger-shaped short-rooted carrot is 'Amerstam Forcing', followed by 'Early Nantes.' Intermediate carrots are typically carrot-shaped, either stump-rooted or tapered to a fine point. 'Chantenay Red Cored', 'Royal Chantenay' and 'Nantes Tip Top' are traditional choices; 'Autumn King' is one of the largest. 'St. Valery' and 'New Red Intermediate' are the two long-rooted varieties on offer, both challenges to the garden perfectionist.

Carrot
'Nantes Tip Top'

# CAULIFLOWERS

Cauliflower is the princess of brassicas, in taste and temperament. It demands near-perfect growing conditions and produces a relatively small crop for the space, time and effort involved.

Although they all look much the same, summer and early autumn cauliflowers are generally tender, while many so-called winter and spring cauliflowers are technically a form of hardy heading broccoli.

**Site and soil**
Provide a rich, neutral or slightly alkaline, well drained soil. Dig in well rotted compost the autumn before planting and incorporate lime, if necessary, in midwinter. A week before planting rake in general-purpose fertilizer. Sun and shelter are essential for over-wintering crops. Avoid frost pockets and never follow one brassica crop with another. (Cauliflowers are particularly prone to pests and diseases.)

**Cultivation**
Never sow sooner than the time recommended on the seed packet. Early summer cauliflower can be sown under glass in early autumn, and the seedlings moved to a cold frame or open ground protected with cloches, then planted out in early spring. Most people, though, sow the seed under glass in late winter or early spring, then transplant in late spring or early summer.

Cauliflower
'Autumn Giant'

80

# CAULIFLOWERS

Cauliflower
'English Winter'

Either way use seed compost initially, and provide a temperature of 10°C (50°F). Once the seedlings germinate, gradually lower the temperature to prevent weak growth. Prick out the seedlings when they are large enough to handle, spacing them 5cm (2in) apart in each direction. Harden off before planting out.

Later summer and autumn crops are sown in seed drills in mid- and late spring, to be transplanted in early summer; winter cauliflowers are sown in late spring and transplanted in midsummer. Sow the seed thinly, in seed drills 15mm (½in) deep and 15cm (6in) apart. Cover with soil, firm and keep well watered. Later, thin to 5-7.5cm (2-3in) apart.

To transplant, whether from under glass or seed beds, wait until plants are about 10cm (4in) high, and water thoroughly the day before transplanting. Lift with plenty of soil around the roots.

Plant firmly, spaced 45-60cm (18-24in) apart in each direction for summer and autumn types, and 75cm (30in) apart for winter and spring ones. Keep weed free and well watered; any check to their growth will result in the formation of tiny, premature heads. Mulch summer and autumn types or feed with nitrogenous fertilizer a month or so after transplanting. Earth up the stems of winter and spring sorts in autumn and feed with quick-acting fertilizer in late winter.

As well as the problems faced by other brassicas (see Broccoli, Cabbages, Brussels

Cauliflower
'Purple Cape'

Sprouts and Kale), cabbage aphids, or mealy aphids, feed on leaf undersides. As the adults overwinter on old brassica stalks, it is essential to destroy the stalks after harvesting. Infested leaves are yellow and blistered; spray with an insecticide suitable for crops.

## Harvesting and storing

Harvest cauliflowers before they are fully developed; that is, when the curds are visible but before they have opened and become discoloured. The transition from the ideal state to the over-ripe one is quick, especially in hot weather, so inspect plants regularly.

Floret development can be retarded by tying the outer leaves loosely round the curds with raffia, or breaking the midribs of the outer leaves and folding them over the curds. Both methods shield the curds from light and air (and, incidentally, can be used to shield overwintering sorts from frost.) Entire plants can be dug up and hung, upside down, in a cool, frost-free spot, where they will keep for two or three weeks. Cauliflower is ideal for freezing and will keep for a week or more refrigerated.

## Varieties

Cauliflowers listed as cropping in one season often straddle the end of the previous season and the beginning of the next. Compact summer cauliflowers include the favourite 'All the Year Round' and its new rival 'Dok'; the small, very early 'Snowball' and the larger 'Dominant'. Autumn varieties are either very large – 'Autumn Giant' and 'Superlative Self Protecting' – or compact and Australian in origin, such as 'Canberra', 'Brisbane' and 'Barrier Reef'. The winter varieties are usually ready in spring. These are the hardiest, and easiest to grow. 'English Winter', the purple-headed 'Purple Cape' and the Dutch 'Walcheren Winter' are typical. The French Roscoff strain of winter cauliflower is hardy only in mild, maritime districts.

# CELERIAC

Celeriac, or turnip-rooted celery, has a small but devoted following among gardeners and cooks. It can be used to make soups or served raw in salads, grated or cut into long, thin strips; since it tends to discolour when cut, a few drops of lemon juice should be added to the cooking water or salad. Celeriac is a close relative of celery and has a similar taste, but it is a less demanding crop and provides an unusual alternative to the more common winter root vegetables.

## Site and soil
Choose a sunny spot and enrich the soil with well rotted compost the autumn before planting. Celeriac will grow in less-than-ideal conditions, but crops will be proportionally smaller. A week before planting, rake in a general-purpose fertilizer.

## Cultivation
Celeriac is slow growing and should be started under glass in early spring. Sow thinly in trays filled with seed compost, or sow two or three seeds per peat pot. Provide a temperature of 13°C (55°F) or slightly higher. Seedlings should appear within two weeks. As soon as they are large enough to handle, prick out or thin those in trays to 4cm (1½in) apart. If growing in peat pots, remove all but the strongest seedling from each of the pots.

Celeriac

83

# CELERIAC

In mid-spring, start to harden off the seedlings, then plant out in late spring, spaced 30-45cm (12-18in) apart in each direction. Plant the swelling base level with the soil, not beneath it. Firm the soil around each plant and water. thoroughly. Hoe or hand weed to keep weed competition down. If slugs are a problem, scatter slug pellets near the plants. Feed weekly with dilute liquid fertilizer from midsummer to mid-autumn. Remove any side shoots that begin to sprout towards the end of summer, and remove any lower leaves that shade the crown. In mid-autumn earth up the base to protect from frost.

**Harvesting and storing**
Lift celeriac from late autumn onwards, as it is needed. (Young, immature celeriac has no special culinary merit.) If prolonged frost threatens or the soil is heavy, lift the whole crop, then twist off any remaining foliage and store the swollen bases in boxes of peat in a cool, frost-free place. Celeriac keeps for two weeks refrigerated, and can be blanched and frozen.

**Varieties**
There are several very similar varieties for sale. 'Marble Ball', 'Claudia', 'Globus' and 'Tellus' are equally reliable.

# CELERY

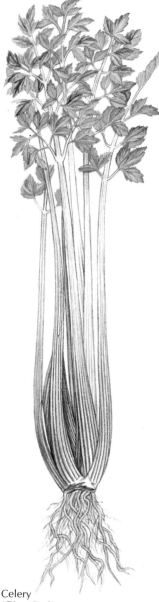

Celery 'Giant Red'

Celery is a definite challenge to grow; in fact, there is a long tradition of celery clubs in the North of England, with annual competitions to find the most perfect specimen. Although modern, self-blanching varieties have eliminated the arduous task of earthing up, they are still a specialist crop and need near-perfect conditions to do well.

## Site and soil

Wild celery grows by the sides of streams and ditches, where there is abundant moisture but well drained, rich soil. Although cultivated celery bears little resemblance to wild celery, the ideal conditions are the same. In traditional crop rotation celery follows onions, potatoes, peas or beans.

For old-fashioned celery, dig a trench, 45cm (18in) wide and 30cm (12in) deep, in the autumn in a sunny spot. Fork over the bottom of the trench to ensure good drainage, then add a layer of well rotted compost about 7.5cm (3in) thick. Return 15cm (6in) of soil to the trench, neatly ridging the remaining soil on either side. (A quick growing crop such as lettuce can be grown on the ridges until they are needed for earthing up.) One week before planting, rake a general-purpose fertilizer into the soil.

Self-blanching celery needs equally rich soil, but finished level with the surrounding ground.

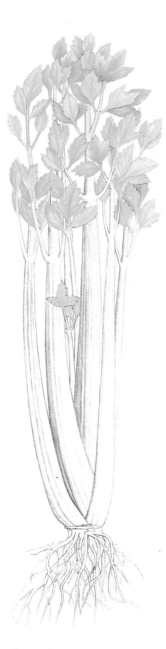

Celery
'Golden Self-Blanching'

## Cultivation

Start celery under glass in early or mid-spring. Sow thinly in trays filled with seed compost and provide a temperature of 16°C (60°F). When the seedlings are large enough to handle, thin or prick out to 5cm (2in) apart in each direction. Celery has very brittle roots, so handle carefully. Begin lowering the temperature, then harden off and plant out in late spring or early summer when six leaves have formed.

Young plants can be bought at garden centres; make sure they have been properly hardened off before planting out.

Water the ground thoroughly before planting. Space old-fashioned celery 22.5cm (9in) apart in rows, and self-blanching 22.5cm (9in) apart in blocks, so that the plants shade one another. Cloche or protect with straw if night frost threatens.

Keep weed free, remove any side shoots that form and provide a steady supply of water, or the plants will bolt. Begin blanching old-fashioned celery in late summer, when the plants are about 30cm (12in) high. First, check that the plants are slug-free and dry, then wrap in cardboard or newspaper, tied with raffia, to keep soil out of the spaces between the stalks. Gradually mound up soil around the plants until, by mid-autumn, only the leaves are visible. Slope the sides of the mounded soil neatly to throw off rain. Protect from frost with a layer of straw or bracken.

Self-blanching celery still benefits from shade when fully grown. The space between the plants can be filled with straw, or a frame of poles and sacking can be placed around the edge of the planting block to provide shade.

Maggots of the celery fly are the most severe problem; if blistered leaves appear, remove and burn them, and spray the crop with malathion.

**Harvesting and storing**

Self-blanching celery is not hardy and should be lifted before the first frost. Work from the outside in, systematically continuing to provide shade. Harvest trench celery methodically along the row, removing the soil until the base of the plant is visible, then levering it out with a fork. Celery keeps for three or four days refrigerated, but does not freeze well.

**Varieties**

Mild-tasting, relatively stringless and frost-tender, the self-blanching celery includes the early 'Golden Self-Blanching', the more flavoursome, yellow-stalked 'Lathom Self-Blanching' and the late 'American Green', harvested in mid-autumn.

Trench celery includes the traditional favourite 'Giant White' and less temperamental 'Dwarf White', both harvested in early winter, and the midwinter 'Giant Pink' and 'Giant Red'.

Blanching celery

# CHARD

Chard

Red-stemmed ruby chard and white-stemmed Swiss chard are botanically related to sugar beet, although they are grown only for their leaves. They are cooked like spinach, though the succulent midribs of Swiss chard can be treated like asparagus. Chard is not often sold in the shops as it wilts quickly once harvested.

### Site and soil
Much less temperamental than spinach, and less likely to bolt, chard will grow well in most free-draining soils, in sun or light shade. Ideally, well rotted compost should be incorporated in the autumn before sowing and, a week before, a general-purpose fertilizer raked into the surface of the soil.

### Cultivation
Like beet, each 'seed' is actually a capsule containing several seeds and is large enough to sow individually. Sow the seed successionally from mid-spring to midsummer, where it is to mature. Make the drills 15mm (½in) deep and 45cm (18in) apart, and space the seeds 10cm (4in) apart. Cover with soil, then firm. Germination should take about two weeks. Thin to one seedling per station and, gradually, to 30cm (12in) apart; these later thinnings can be used in the kitchen.

Chard
'Ruby Chard'

Hoe to keep weeds down and water generously in dry weather. Mulching with well rotted compost helps keep weeds down and retain soil moisture. Feed the growing plants from time to time with dilute applications of liquid fertilizer. Any flower buds that start to form should be removed. Slugs can be troublesome, so scatter slug pellets around the plants.

## Harvesting and storing

By sowing successionally and protecting late crops with straw, bracken, or cloches, chard can be harvested from midsummer through to the following summer. Begin picking the outer leaves when the plants are 37.5-45cm (15-18in) tall. Cut with a sharp knife near the base of the plant, leaving the inner crown intact to continue producing new leaves. Never disturb the roots or strip a plant entirely.

Harvest regularly, and remove any old, tough leaves which may have been missed earlier; if left on the plant, they inhibit further production of young leaves. These old leaves are too strong flavoured to be of use in the kitchen.

Chard doesn't freeze, or store particularly well in the refrigerator for more than a day or two.

## Varieties

'Ruby Chard' or 'Rhubarb Chard' has dark, wrinkled leaves and crimson stems, and is attractive enough to be grown in a flower border. 'Swiss Chard', 'Silver Beet' or 'Seakale Beet' has striking, fleshy white midribs and veins.

# CHICORY

Chicory
Blanched chicon

For most people, chicory means the beautiful, plump, pale chicons forced in autumn for winter and spring salads. But there are also non-forcing types, resembling cos lettuces; hardier than lettuce, they are grown for harvesting in mid- and late autumn. Chicory has a slightly bitter taste, refreshing rather than unpleasant.

**Site and soil**
A sunny spot and well drained, light but reasonably rich soil is required. (Shallow, stony and very acid soils are unsuitable.) Enrich with compost the autumn before sowing, lime in midwinter, if necessary, and rake in general-purpose fertilizer about a week before sowing.

**Cultivation**
Sow in late spring or early summer for forcing varieties, and early or midsummer for non-forcing ones. (Starting sooner than this usually leads to bolting.) Sow thinly, where it is to grow, in drills 15mm (½in) deep and 25-30cm (10-12in) apart. Thin seedlings of forcing varieties to 15cm (6in) apart, and non-forcing varieties to 25cm (10in) apart.

Keep weeds down, and net the rows if birds are troublesome. Scatter slug pellets near the plants. Should any plants try to flower, remove the flower stem.

In late autumn, carefully lift the roots of forcing varieties. Save only those that are unforked, and with a diameter at the top of 2.5-5cm (1-2in). Cut the foliage back to 2.5cm (1in) above the crown, and cut the roots back to 15-20cm (6-8in). Store horizontally in boxes of damp sand, placed in a cool, dark place, until you need them. (Leaving the roots in the ground is risky; they may sprout in mild weather or become inaccessible in a hard frost.)

Force a few roots at a time, packing them vertically in a large, peat-filled box or pot; the crowns should be just visible. Cover with an upturned pot, its drainage hole taped to exclude light, or place in a large polythene bag. Provide a minimum temperature of 10°C (50°F) and water very lightly.

## Harvesting and storing

Cut non-forcing varieties from mid-autumn onwards; protecting them with cloches or straw extends the cropping period into winter. It takes about a month for forced chicons to develop fully; they should be 15-20cm (6-8in) long. Pull up the roots and cut the chicons as close to the base as possible. Place new roots in the pot, cover and repeat the process. If you have sufficient roots, forcing can continue until early spring.

## Varieties

'Witloof' ('Belgian Chicory') is the standard forcing variety, but its heads are loose and open unless forced through a thick layer of peat. 'Normato' is an early Dutch forcing variety, which is naturally tight headed. The favourite non-forcing variety is 'Sugar Loaf' ('Pain de Sucre'). The trendiest, most *nouvelle cuisine* of the lot is red chicory, or *rossa de Verona*; when blanched, it forms tight-headed lettuce-like radicchio.

Radicchio
(Rossa de Verona)

# CORN SALAD

Corn salad, or lamb's lettuce, has a slightly bitter taste and a certain rarity value. A leaf or two in a salad is invariably, almost reverentially, noted on a restaurant menu. In fact, it is a quick, easy vegetable and grows wild in corn fields and hedge banks.

### Site and soil
Choose a sunny, sheltered spot with rich, free-draining soil. Corn salad makes a good catch crop between slower-growing vegetables; it could follow peas or broad beans.

### Cultivation
Corn salad is hardy and can be sown successively from late winter onwards, but it is most valuable if sown in midsummer or late summer for autumn and winter cropping. Sow thinly in drills 15mm (½in) deep and 15cm (6in) apart. Hoe or hand weed to keep weeds down, scatter slug pellets and net against birds. Keep well watered and thin the seedlings to 15cm (6in) apart. (Use the thinnings in the kitchen.) Cloching late crops, or protecting them from frost with straw, keeps them growing and tender, for longer.

Corn salad

### Harvesting and storing
Whole plants can be harvested like lettuce, or a succession of young leaves picked once the plant has produced eight or ten leaves. Don't strip a plant if you want more leaves – take only two or three at a time.

# CUCUMBERS

Growing greenhouse, or
frame, cucumbers is not an
exercise to be undertaken
lightly. These climbers need
more heat and humidity than
most other greenhouse crops –
in the past they were given a
greenhouse of their own – and
they also need a great deal of
care, attention and cossetting.

Easier is the outdoor, or
ridge, cucumber, so called
because it was traditionally
grown on ridges of manure.
Conventional ridge cucumbers
are usually shorter and rougher
looking than their dark-green,
slender, symmetrical and
almost unnaturally perfect
greenhouse counterparts.
Japanese varieties of ridge
cucumber, however, combine
the appearance of greenhouse
ones with the ease of
cultivation of ridge ones.

In the kitchen, cucumber
can be cooked, rather like
marrow or courgette to which
it is related. Most people prefer
cucumber cool, fresh and
unadulterated, in a vinaigrette,
or a yoghurt and fresh mint
dressing.

### Site and soil

For greenhouse cucumbers,
the traditional method was to
make hot beds of fermenting
manure, covered with a good
depth of soil, in the open
ground of a greenhouse or cold
frame. A more modern
approach is to grow two plants
per grow bag, or individual
plants in 25-30cm (10-12in)
diameter pots filled with John

Cucumbers

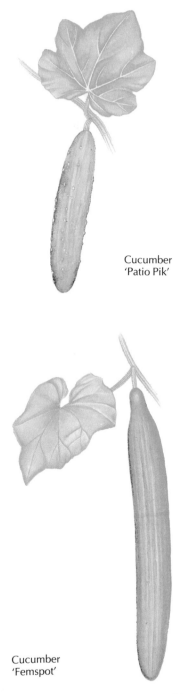

Cucumber
'Patio Pik'

Cucumber
'Femspot'

Innes potting compost No. 3; these methods eliminate the risk of pests or diseases building up in the soil. For ordinary greenhouse cucumbers a minimum temperature of 16°C (60°F) is needed; and for all-female varieties a minimum temperature of 21°C (70°F).

Cucumbers growing outdoors need a very rich, well drained soil, full sun and shelter. In early or mid-spring, dig out a hole 37.5cm (15in) square and deep and fill it with a mixture of well rotted compost and soil, leaving it slightly mounded on top. If growing more than one plant, space the holes 1.2m (4ft) apart. A week before sowing or planting, rake in a general-purpose fertilizer.

**Cultivation**
Sow greenhouse cucumber seed under glass, in late winter or early spring in a heated greenhouse, and in mid-spring in an unheated greenhouse. Outdoor varieties can also be started under glass in mid-spring and planted out in late spring, after the last frost.

Sow seed individually in 7.5cm (3in) peat pots. Place the seed on its side in the compost, 15mm (½in) deep. Provide a minimum temperature of 21°C (70°F); germination takes from three to nine days. Keep well watered, and maintain high humidity and a high temperature for all-female greenhouse cucumbers; seedlings of ordinary greenhouse cucumbers tolerate 16°C (60°F), and outdoor cucumbers should gradually be

Cucumber
'Venlo Pickling'

Cucumber
'Crystal Apple'

exposed to lower temperatures and hardened off.

Transplant heated greenhouse varieties into pots or grow bags in early or mid-spring; unheated varieties in late spring. Cucumber plants have very fragile root systems and should be disturbed as little as possible.

Whether placing the peat pot in a larger pot, a grow bag or the open ground, firm the surrounding soil or compost and water thoroughly after planting. (Young ridge cucumbers may need protection from night frosts for a week or two after planting.)

You can also sow ridge cucumbers in situ in late spring; sow two or three seeds, on edge, 2.5cm (1in) deep and well spaced out, in the middle of each prepared mound. Cloche or otherwise protect from frost. When the seedlings are large enough to handle, remove all but the strongest from each mound.

Training is different for greenhouse and ridge cucumbers. For greenhouse cucumbers, make a wire support system. Fix three wires, running horizontally and 30cm (12in) from the glass; the bottom wire should be 15cm (6in) above the pot or grow bag; the top wire 2.1m (7ft) high, and the middle wire half-way between. Fix a stout bamboo pole vertically next to each plant, securing it to the wires. As the young plant grows tie it to the stake, then pinch out the growing point when it reaches the upper wire. Pinch out the side shoots two leaves beyond female

Pinching out the tops of ridge cucumbers

Cucumber
'Burpless Tasty Green'

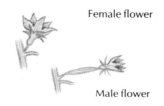

Female flower

Male flower

flowers, which have tiny cucumbers behind the petals. Pinch out non-flowering side shoots when 60cm (2ft) long. Train side shoots along the horizontal wires.

With ridge cucumbers the growing tips should be pinched out after the sixth leaf is produced. Train out the resulting side shoots evenly spaced over the mound, stopping them after the sixth or seventh leaf. Some Japanese varieties need vertical supports of stout stakes, netting and straining wires, like those for runner beans. Train greenhouse cucumbers growing in a cold frame in much the same way, training the side shoots that form after the initial pinching out into the four corners of the frame and stopping the side shoots as necessary.

Both greenhouse and ridge cucumbers need a steady supply of water, but will quickly rot in waterlogged conditions. Damp down the greenhouse twice a day to maintain high humidity, but don't spray indoor plants directly. Lightly spray the foliage of ridge cucumbers in dry weather.

Remove the male cucumbers – the ones with narrow stalks behind the petals – from traditional varieties of greenhouse cucumber, and also any stray male flowers sometimes produced on 'all female' varieties. Fertilized female greenhouse cucumbers are misshapen, full of hard seeds and bitter. Leave the male flowers on outdoor ridge varieties, as the female flowers must be pollinated if they are to crop.

Feed both outdoor and ridge cucumbers once the fruit start swelling with a high nitrogenous feed, such as tomato fertilizer. Protect the fruit of ridge cucumbers from the soil with a pane of glass, slate, or sheet of black polythene.

There are many possible problems, but the most serious is cucumber mosaic virus, which shows up as yellow, mottled leaves and small, mis-shapen fruit. Lift and destroy infected plants, and control aphids which transmit the disease. Red spider mite is the most troublesome pest, particularly in dry atmospheric conditions. At the first sign of bronzed leaves or silky webbing, spray with malathion or derris.

## Harvesting and storing
Greenhouse cucumbers are usually harvested from early summer to mid-autumn; outdoor cucumbers from late summer to mid-autumn. Cut cucumbers, using a sharp knife, before they reach their maximum size; fully mature and over-mature cucumbers inhibit further fruit production if left on the plant, and taste bitter and seedy. Greenhouse and Japanese cucumbers should be parallel-sided and 30-37.5cm (12-15in) long. (The Victorian standard of excellence was nine times the diameter long and as straight-sided as a ruler.)

The optimum size for other outdoor cucumbers varies from 7.5cm (3in) for apple cucumbers to 22.5cm (9in) for some standard ridge varieties. The smaller-growing types, gherkins, are best picked when 10cm (4in) long.

Cucumbers don't freeze, but will keep refrigerated for a week. Gherkins are traditionally pickled, but cucumbers are also a fine basis for chutneys and relishes, marrying especially well with apple and onion.

## Varieties
Traditional varieties include the old-fashioned 'Telegraph'; 'Conqueror', suitable for unheated greenhouses; the slightly ribbed, medium-sized 'Butcher's Disease Resisting' and the pale-skinned, deliciously flavoured 'Sigmadew'.

Greenhouse $F_1$ 'all female' varieties – prolific, disease resistant, but small and heat loving – include the very popular 'Pepinex' and compact 'Pepita', with 15cm (6in) fruit; and the early cropping 'Femspot'.

Outdoor varieties include the traditional 'Venlo Pickling' gherkin and the earlier and reputedly higher yielding 'Hokus' gherkin. 'Crystal Apple' is the standard round pale variety. Traditional ridge cucumbers include the virus-resistant $F_1$ hybrid 'Marion'; the vigorous and tolerant $F_1$ 'Burpee Hybrid'; the dwarf-growing 'Patio Pik', and the mildew-resistant, self-descriptive, 'Burpless Tasty Green'. 'Kyoto' and 'Chinese Long Green' are the most widely grown Japanese varieties.

# DANDELIONS

The leaves of this well known perennial weed can make a valuable contribution to the kitchen. Mature leaves are too bitter to be eaten unless they are blanched by forcing first, but young leaves can be used in salads or steamed and served as a vegetable. The flowers are traditionally made into wine and the ground-up roots make a rather dubious substitute for coffee.

**Site and soil**
Choose a semi-shaded site with reasonably fertile, well drained soil.

**Cultivation**
Sow in situ in mid-spring, in drills 15mm (½in) deep and 30cm (12in) apart. Thin the seedlings to 20cm (8in) apart. Keep well watered and weeded, and remove any flower buds that may appear.

The long thick roots can be lifted in autumn and brought indoors for forcing, like those of chicory. Pack tightly and vertically in boxes filled with peat, and keep in a cool, totally dark place. Water lightly from time to time.

Alternatively, the plants can stay in the open ground and the following spring the leaves covered with an upturned flower pot or box from which all light is excluded.

Dandelion

**Harvesting and storing**
Modest cropping of young leaves can take place from early summer. Those forced in boxes indoors take three or four weeks, after which the roots should be discarded. It takes about two weeks to blanch the leaves of plants growing outdoors. Stop blanching in early summer to allow the plants to build up strength for future crops.

# ENDIVE

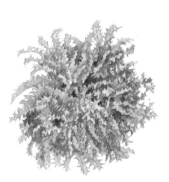

Endive
'Moss Curled'

Endive and chicory are sometimes confused: the French for endive is *chicorée frisée*, and for chicory it is *endive*. Like chicory, endive is an unusual salad vegetable with more taste and character than lettuce, and it is available in late autumn and winter when lettuce is finished. Like chicory, endive is rather bitter unless blanched, and though it can be braised like chicory it is nicest served in its crisp and piquant fresh state.

**Site and soil**
Choose a deep, rich, well drained soil. Incorporate well rotted manure in the autumn before sowing; a week before sowing, rake in general-purpose fertilizer. Endive sown in spring for late summer cropping needs light shade to prevent it bolting; if sown in summer and autumn it needs sun, to help it survive low temperatures in autumn and winter.

**Cultivation**
Sow curly-leaved endive from mid-spring until late summer. Sow the hardier broad-leaved endive from midsummer to early autumn. Sow thinly in drills 15mm (½in) deep and 37.5cm (15in) apart. Seedlings should appear within a week. As soon as they are large enough to handle, thin the plants to 30cm (12in) apart.

Keep weeded and watered; an erratic water supply can lead to bolting. A thick mulch

Endive
'Batavian Green'

over damp soil helps retain moisture and keeps weed growth down.

About two months after sowing, feed with a liquid fertilizer and continue feeding regularly until the plants are fully grown. Start blanching then, but only a few plants at a time for a fully blanched endive will rot if left indefinitely. Endive blanched when wet will also rot.

There are several ways to blanch: the easiest is to tie the leaves together with raffia towards the top of the plant, then enclose them in a large, upturned flower pot, its hole plugged to exclude light. Endive is naturally flat and can also be blanched by being covered with a large plate, tile or, traditionally a plank of wood to cover several plants. Slugs, like people, prefer the blanched leaves, so scatter pellets nearby. Late crops, particularly of curly-leaved endive, benefit from autumn cloching.

Late crops can also be lifted and planted in shallow boxes of peat, then placed to blanch in a cold, dark place, such as a shed or under darkened greenhouse staging.

**Harvesting and storing**
Blanching indoors takes from three to six weeks and is faster in warmer weather. Harvest the pale-centred plants by cutting off cleanly at the base. Endive keeps for two or three days refrigerated but is unsuitable for freezing.

**Varieties**
'Moss Curled' and 'Green Curled' are curly-leaved forms with attractive, finely divided foliage. Broad-leaved, round-leaved or Batavian endive is usually sold as 'Batavian Green'.

# FENNEL, FLORENCE

Florence fennel, sweet fennel or finocchio is a close relative of the common fennel herb, but it is grown for its aniseed flavoured, swollen leaf base – a rounded, bulbous version of celery. Its bright-green, thread-like foliage is similarly flavoured and makes a pretty garnish for savoury dishes. Florence fennel is widely grown in Italy where it is served fresh in salads and antipasti, braised or grilled, or as a stuffing for rich meats. In cooler climates, it is a temperamental crop.

**Site and soil**
Choose the warmest, sunniest patch, such as the base of a south-facing wall. Sandy, well drained soil is best; enrich it with well rotted compost the autumn before sowing and, if the soil is acid, lime in midwinter. (Poor, badly drained, heavy and acid soils are unsuitable and crops are certain to fail in such conditions.) A week before sowing, rake in a general-purpose fertilizer.

**Cultivation**
For a steady supply, sow fennel successively where it is to grow from mid-spring to late summer. For early sowings use cloches to warm up the soil for a week or two beforehand. Make the drills 15mm (½in) deep and 45cm (18in) apart. Water lightly, sow thinly, and when the seedlings appear, thin to 25cm (10in) apart.

Florence fennel

Again, for early sowings, it is a good idea to protect the young plants, especially when night frosts threaten.

Keep weed free and provide a steady supply of water; uneven supplies are liable to result in the plants running to seed before the swollen bases form. Mulching the ground with garden compost or covering with a sheet of black plastic, after thoroughly watering, helps conserve soil moisture and thwarts weeds.

When the bases begin swelling, give an additional feed of general-purpose fertilizer. Begin drawing up the soil round the bases when they are egg-sized to blanch them. Do it gradually and continue until the bases are ready for harvesting, about a month later. Cloche late crops.

Though demanding in terms of weather, feeding and watering, Florence fennel is generally pest and disease free.

**Harvesting and storing**
Begin harvesting from midsummer onwards when the bases are about 10cm (4in) across. Either fork up or cut at ground level, where the base joins the roots.

Fennel does not keep for long in the refrigerator, but it can be blanched and frozen – it is rarely necessary to do this though, since bumper crops of fennel are most unlikely in cool temperate climates.

**Varieties**
Most are sold as 'Sweet Fennel' or 'Florence Fennel'. The variety 'Sirio' is quick growing and best sown in midsummer.

# GOOD KING HENRY

This little known perennial was more popular in the past, when it was grown as a pot herb and vegetable for its medicinal value. Today, it grows wild on roadside verges and pastures but is rather more difficult to find in seed catalogues. Its young shoots are peeled, boiled and eaten as asparagus, and its leaves boiled and served like spinach. It has several common names, including poor man's asparagus and mercury.

### Site and soil
Though it is tolerant of poor soils, it prefers a reasonably fertile one, enriched with well rotted compost in the autumn before sowing. Remove every trace of perennial weed to prevent trouble later on. Sun or light shade is preferable.

### Cultivation
Sow where it is to grow in spring; make the drills 15mm (½in) deep and 45cm (18in) apart. When the seedlings appear, thin to 30cm (12in) apart. It is best not to pick any leaves or shoots the first growing season; simply keep weed free and well watered. In autumn, cut down the above-ground growth and mulch with well rotted compost. The following spring harvesting can begin. Older plants are best replaced after three or four years, either from seed or by lifting and dividing existing plants.

### Harvesting and storing
From mid-spring to early summer pick the young shoots, then stop to allow the plants to build up reserves. The spinach-like leaves can be picked in moderate amounts until the end of summer.

Good King Henry

# HAMBURG PARSLEY

This unusual biennial is grown for its white, parsnip-like roots, which taste like parsnip mixed with celeriac, and for its coarse leaves which can be used like parsley. In the kitchen, the roots are scrubbed, sliced, then boiled or deep fried. In the garden, its main attraction is its shade tolerance.

**Site and soil**
Choose a free-draining soil, enriched with well rotted compost the autumn before sowing. Freshly enriched and stony soils are unsuitable since they cause the roots to fork.

**Cultivation**
Sow thinly, where it is to grow, in early or mid-spring in drills 15mm (½in) deep and 25cm (10in) apart. Germination is slow and cloching early sowings warms up the soil and speeds up the process. Thin the seedlings to 25cm (10in) apart. Water in dry weather and keep weeded. Sometimes the half-grown roots lift themselves part-way out of the ground; if this happens, draw the soil up around them. Pests and diseases are rare.

**Harvesting and storing**
Harvest the leaves sparingly; never strip any one plant. In mid- or late autumn, begin lifting the roots which should be about 20cm (8in) long. In mild areas the crop can be left in the ground until needed; otherwise, lift and store like carrots in boxes of sand or peat.

Hamburg parsley

# KALE

Kale
'Tall Green Curled'

Kale
Plain leaved

Kale's main claim to fame is its tough constitution and frost hardiness. Unfortunately its use as cattle fodder tarnishes its image in the kitchen. While some of the older varieties, and old leaves of all varieties, are fierce in flavour, newly picked young shoots are more acceptable and mild. Kale and ham, bacon or pork are a traditional culinary combination, particularly in winter and early spring when the vegetable garden is bare.

## Site and soil
Kale is not fussy, provided the soil is well drained and not too acid. Lime in midwinter if necessary, and about a week before planting apply a general-purpose fertilizer. In crop rotation, kale can follow lettuce, peas, beans or early new potatoes – never another brassica. Full sun and shelter are desirable as the crop has to overwinter and some forms are quite tall; avoid low-lying frost pockets.

## Cultivation
Except for rape kale, which is sown where it matures, sow kale in seed beds in mid-spring for transplanting in midsummer. Make the drills 15mm (½in) deep and 15cm (6in) apart. Sow thinly, cover and firm (firm ground is essential with all brassicas). Water if dry, keep weeded and thin seedlings to 5-7.5cm (2-3in) apart before they become crowded.

# KALE

Transplant to their permanent position in midsummer. Water the seed bed thoroughly the day before transplanting, then lift the plants with as much soil as possible clinging to the roots, and plant 45-60cm (18-24in) apart in each direction. The plants should be a little deeper than they were in the seed bed. Water, and keep watered in dry weather. Hoe to keep weeds down and to stop the surface from compacting.

In autumn, earth up soil around the roots; tall-growing sorts or those on exposed sites may need staking as well for added stability. In early spring, apply a quick-acting nitrogenous fertilizer to encourage new growth. After harvesting, dig up and burn old stalks as many brassica pests overwinter on them. Mealy aphid is one; it can be found on leaf undersides from early summer onwards, causing infested leaves to yellow and wilt. Spray with a suitable insecticide. (See also Broccoli, Brussels Sprouts, Cabbages and Cauliflowers.)

**Harvesting and storing**
Wait until all the other vegetables in the garden are finished and at least one frost has softened kale's flavour. From late autumn onwards pick the tender leaves from the crown, then take the succulent side shoots, working down from the top as needed through mid-spring. Kale keeps for two or three days refrigerated, or can be blanched and frozen.

**Varieties**
Curly-leaved, or Scotch, kale is the most popular; it includes the dwarf 'Spurt' and 'Frosty', and the old-fashioned 'Tall Green Curled'. Hardier but coarser is plain-leaved kale: 'Thousand Headed' and 'Cottagers'. 'Hungry Gap' is the standard rape kale variety. 'Pentland Brig' is half-way between curly- and plain-leaved; it produces broccoli-like spears as well as leafy crowns and side shoots.

Kale
'Pentland Brig'

# KOHL RABI

A little known relative of the turnip, kohl rabi is a biennial grown as an annual for its swollen stem base or globe. With its curiously sparse, long-stemmed leaves, the globe, which sits on the surface of the soil, resembles a tiny, newly landed space ship; a whole row of them has an endearing charm. Its flavour is variously described as nutty, celery-like, turnip-like and cabbage-like.

Kohl rabi has no real identity in the kitchen, and is used like turnip. Trim off the roots and leaves, then scrub and boil the globe until tender. (The leaves can also be boiled and served.) Grated raw kohl rabi makes a refreshing addition to a salad, and the flavour of cooked kohl rabi complements winter casseroles and soups.

**Site and soil**
Kohl rabi is far more tolerant of mediocre conditions than turnip, though very heavy, acid and waterlogged soils are unsuitable. A sunny spot and neutral or slightly alkaline soil are best. Incorporate well rotted compost in the autumn before sowing, and lime in midwinter if necessary. About a week before sowing, rake in a general-purpose fertilizer. Because kohl rabi is quick growing, taking two to three months from sowing to harvesting, it is a good catch crop. Being a brassica, it should not follow other brassicas in crop rotation.

Kohl rabi
'Purple Vienna'

# KOHL RABI

Kohl rabi
'Green Vienna'

### Cultivation
Sow kohl rabi where it is to
grow, from early spring to early
summer for cropping in late
summer and early autumn, and
in mid- or late summer for late
autumn crops. Successional
sowing is important because
the globes must be harvested
when they are still immature,
otherwise they quickly become
woody and unpleasant tasting.
Sow thinly in drills 15mm
(½in) deep and 30cm (12in)
apart. Cover, firm and water if
the soil is dry. Thin the
seedlings to 15cm (6in) apart.
Keep weed free by hoeing or
hand weeding, and protect
from birds which are fond of
the young leaves. Keep well
watered, especially in dry
weather. Cloche late crops in
autumn.

Though a brassica, kohl rabi
is not normally troubled by the
pests and diseases associated
with that family. Use slug
pellets if slugs are troublesome,
and if cabbage root fly is a
problem sprinkle bromophos
on the soil before planting.

### Harvesting and storing
Lift the crop when 5-7.5cm (2-
3in) in diameter.
Unfortunately, it can't be
stored in boxes in a cool shed.
Either refrigerate for up to two
weeks, or blanch and freeze.

### Varieties
For early crops, choose either
the green-skinned 'Green
Vienna' or the pale-green-
skinned 'White Vienna'. Both
are white fleshed, as is the
purple-skinned 'Purple
Vienna', suitable for autumn
cropping.

# LAND CRESS

In the kitchen, land cress, also called American cress and winter cress, is used exactly like its aquatic cousin, watercress; it is perfect for salads, soups, sandwiches and garnishes. In the garden, however, this hardy perennial is much easier to grow as lavish supplies of water are unnecessary.

**Site and soil**
Light shade and rich, damp soil are best. In the autumn before sowing, work in plenty of well rotted compost. Because land cress is a long-term crop, every trace of perennial weed must be eradicated as part of the soil preparation.

**Cultivation**
Sow thinly in drills, where it is to grow, from late spring for summer crops to late summer for autumn and winter crops. Make the drills 15mm (½in) deep and 30cm (12in) apart, watering the bed first if it is dry. After sowing mark the drills; land cress, in common with many garden weeds, is a *Cruciferae*, and the seedlings look much the same.

As soon as the seedlings are large enough to handle, thin to 20cm (8in) apart; use the thinnings in the kitchen. Keep well watered, scatter slug pellets around the crop and remove any flower stalks that form.

For winter crops, cloche the plants in autumn, and if heavy frost threatens cover the cloches with straw or sacking. Lift and divide the roots every three or four years in spring to renew the crop.

Land cress

**Harvesting and storing**
Pick the outer leaves from the young plants so central growth can continue. Pick the young, central growth from older plants. Use as soon after picking as possible.

# LEEKS

There is something imposing and noble about a well grown leek, as countless leek-growing competitions in the North of England attest. Even today, huge, stumpy pot leeks are displayed, weighed and admired at these events, however tough and tasteless such specimens may be in the kitchen. Both pot and long leeks are biennial relatives of the onion, with a milder flavour, a reputation for health-giving properties and a relatively easy-going nature in the garden. Though less fussy and prone to pests and diseases than onions, leeks do take a long time to reach maturity and also need transplanting and earthing up.

In the kitchen, the elongated white bulb is the main ingredient of classic, cold vichyssoise soup; leeks à la grecque; served cold with a vinaigrette, are equally delicious. They add flavour and substance to stews, casseroles and more humble soups. Overcooking and undercleaning are the main causes of leeks' tarnished reputation at the dining table. Partially slitting, then soaking the leeks before cooking, solves one problem; boiling for no more than eight or ten minutes solves the other.

### Site and soil
Leeks will survive in any soil that is not waterlogged, but they do best on soil that is light, rich but not recently enriched,

Leek
'Lyon Prizetaker'

and firm but not too compacted. If the soil has not been enriched for a previous crop, add well rotted compost the autumn before planting. A week or so before planting rake in a general-purpose fertilizer. Full sun is necessary and shelter, especially for those crops that will overwinter in the open ground.

## Cultivation

Leeks grown for exhibiting in autumn shows are sown under glass in early, mid- or late winter, then hardened off and planted out in late spring. For most people, however, having leeks so early is pointless as the garden is full of summer vegetables then.

It is more sensible to sow outdoors in seed beds in early or mid-spring, then transplant the seedlings to their final position in early summer. For late crops in mid-spring, delay sowing until early midsummer; otherwise the process is the same.

Make the seed drills 15mm (½in) deep and 15cm (6in) apart. Sow the seed thinly, cover with soil and firm; water lightly if necessary. Germination usually takes two or three weeks. Thin the seedlings in gradual stages until they are 5-7.5 cm (2-3in) apart. Keep weed free and well watered.

When the seedlings are about 20cm (8in) high and as thick as a pencil, prepare them for transplanting. (Young plants, ready for planting directly into their final positions, can be bought from garden centres.) Water the

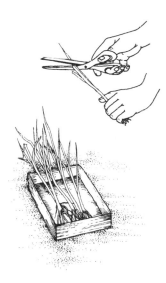

Trimming leeks prior to planting

**Planting out leeks**

seed bed the day before transplanting. Don't pull the plants out; carefully lever them instead, using a garden fork. Trim the roots back to 2.5cm (1in) from the base and trim back the leaves a little as well.

Leeks can be grown on the flat (the system most often used for exhibition growing); in trenches similar to celery trenches; on ridges, if the soil is badly drained; or in individual holes. Most gardeners use the last method, which is a form of self-blanching, as the lower stems are protected from sunlight. Use a wooden dibber to make holes 15cm (6in) deep, about 5cm (2in) in diameter, 15cm (6in) apart, and in rows 25-30cm (10-12in) apart. Lower one plant into each hole, then gently fill the holes with water. Don't fill the holes with soil; nature does it for you in good time.

Hoe to keep down weeds, and water if the soil is dry. Feed with dilute liquid fertilizer every two weeks during the growing season until the end of summer. Thereafter, stop feeding because tough, not lush, growth is needed to withstand winter weather. Unless you are growing for exhibition, cut back any leaves that trail on the ground.

Begin blanching the above-ground growth in early autumn. Gradually earth up dry soil, about 2.5cm (1in) at a time, around the stems. Finish in late autumn. An optional refinement is to protect the stems from the soil by enclosing them in plastic or clay drain pipes, or brown paper tied with twine.

**Puddling in leeks**

# LEEKS

Leeks can be, but rarely are, attacked by the same troubles as onions (see page 126). They do sometimes suffer from fungal infections: white tip turns the leaves white and causes stunted growth, and reddy-brown leek rust can be fatal. Proper crop rotation is the best preventive. Badly infected plants should be lifted and burnt and the remainder sprayed with a fungicide. The caterpillars of leek moth eat through the leaves, leaving only transparent skins. Hand pick and burn infested leaves; spray the remainder with fenitrothion.

**Harvesting and storing**
Leeks are ready from early autumn until the following spring, depending on variety and time of sowing. (Broad flag leeks, or London leeks, are frost tender and must be lifted in autumn.) Lever leeks out as needed, using a garden fork or spade. If the ground is likely to freeze solid, lift leeks in autumn and either store them in boxes of peat in a cool but frost-free spot, or heel them into a sheltered, lightly shaded bit of the garden. Leeks can be refrigerated or frozen.

**Varieties**
Exhibitors choose early varieties such as 'Autumn Mammoth-Early Market', which is frost tender, and the hardier 'Lyon Prizetaker'. Hardy varieties, for harvesting from early to late winter, include the immensely popular pot leek 'Musselburgh' and 'Snowstar', said to be an improved form. Leeks for harvesting from late winter through mid-spring include 'Giant Winter-Royal Favourite', 'Giant Winter-Catalina', and the very hardy 'Winter Crop'.

# LETTUCES

Lettuce
'Lobjoit's Green'

A packet of lettuce seed is probably the first a would-be gardener buys, and tidy rows of lettuce are a predictable summer feature of allotments and back gardens. Lettuce, however, can be a year-round crop, given a suitable selection of varieties and cloching or artificial heat. It is temperamental, especially out of season, but if its needs are met it is quick growing and rewarding. Where space is at a premium, lettuce is ideal as a catch crop or intercrop between slower growing vegetables.

In the kitchen lettuce is the undisputed king of salads, at its best when freshly picked and served raw. Some varieties are tasteless and need the help of a good vinaigrette, or a few leaves of watercress, dandelion or lamb's lettuce to add flavour. Lettuce can be braised or made into soup, but part of its charm is its fresh colour and crisp texture, both of which are lost during cooking.

There are several types of lettuce: the relatively slow-growing, tricky, crisp-leafed upright cos; the round, soft-leafed butterhead, popular, tolerant but a bit characterless; the bolt-resistant, round crispheads; and the heartless, curly, loose-leaf lettuce.

### Site and soil
Lettuce needs a light but fertile, moisture retentive but not waterlogged, neutral or alkaline soil. Well before

Lettuce
'Winter Density'

Lettuce
'Tom Thumb'

sowing, work in plenty of rotted compost, digging the soil deeply as you go. Lime, if necessary, in winter. Before sowing, rake the surface to a fine, crumbly tilth and work in a general-purpose fertilizer.

Early crops need sun and shelter; summer crops need sun or light shade; the latter helps prevent bolting.

**Cultivation**
Getting the timing right with lettuce is half the battle. For a mid-spring crop, sow a winter-hardy variety in early autumn in a mild sheltered garden; or under cloches in mid-autumn in cold gardens. For a late spring crop, sow in peat pots under glass in late winter. Harden off, then plant out under cloches in early spring. For a summer and autumn crop, sow successively every two weeks outdoors from early spring to midsummer. For a late autumn and early winter crop, sow outdoors in late summer and cloche in early autumn. For a mid- and late winter crop, sow under glass in early or mid-autumn and provide a minimum winter temperature of 7°C (45°F).

Sow little and often; once mature, lettuce is quick to bolt and it doesn't freeze.

Lettuce can be transplanted but it is then more likely to bolt; whenever possible, sow lettuce where it is to mature. Make the drills 15mm (½in) deep and 30cm (12in) apart. Sow thinly, cover with soil and firm. Begin thinning once the seedlings are large enough to handle. Water the day before if the soil is dry, then thin

Lettuce
'Webb's Wonderful'

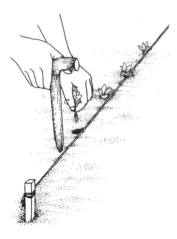

Planting out lettuces

gradually, always firming the remaining plants, until they are 15-30cm (6-12in) apart according to variety. Cos lettuce can also be block sown in rows 10cm (4in) apart and harvested, Continental fashion, as cut greens.

Plant out lettuce started under glass, moved from one bit of the garden to another, or bought from a garden centre, in early or mid-spring. Late spring and summer plantings tend to bolt. Be careful when handling the fine roots as they snap off easily. Plant at half the final spacing; use the thinnings in the kitchen. Plant firmly but not too deeply; if the lower leaves are buried they rot. Water thoroughly after planting.

Sparrows and slugs are fond of young lettuce; protect plants with netting or criss-crossed black cotton and use slug pellets. Water regularly in the daylight hours ; evening watering, when the temperature is falling, encourages grey mould. Hoe to keep weeds down and the soil surface open.

Lettuce grown under glass, and open-grown lettuce in cold weather, need much less watering; too much water encourages disease. Keep lettuce under glass, whether greenhouse, frame or cloche, well ventilated for the same reason.

Over-wintering lettuce appreciates an application of quick-acting fertilizer in early spring.

Lettuce is vulnerable to many pests and diseases but the most probable are aphids,

Lettuce
'Red Salad Bowl'

mosaic virus and grey mould. Aphids cause puckered, sticky leaves and, more seriously, transmit mosaic virus which shows up as yellow, mottled leaves and stunted growth. Destroy infected plants; spray those infested with aphids with a suitable insecticide. Destroy plants infected with the self-descriptive grey mould (which also causes brown, rotten stems) and spray the remainder with thiram.

### Harvesting and storing
As soon as its heart is firm a lettuce is ready. It can of course be harvested before that; but it can't be left much later, or it runs to seed and the leaves become tough and bitter. Old-fashioned gardeners pick lettuce in the morning with the dew on. Butterhead lettuce keeps refrigerated for a couple of days; cos and crisphead slightly longer.

I harvest loose-leaf lettuce like spinach by picking a few outer leaves at a time, leaving the inner leaves to grow on. Cut off the tender young leaves of closely sown cos; the roots will send up a second crop later.

### Varieties
There are dozens. For a small garden buy a pack of mixed seed with different cropping times. Otherwise match the variety chosen to the timing and conditions intended.

There are two loose-leaf varieties: 'Salad Bowl' and the pretty 'Red Salad Bowl' which are both spring sown. Cos varieties include the sweet, late summer or early autumn-sown 'Winter Density'; the large, self-folding 'Lobjoit's Green' and the similar, pale-centred 'Paris White'; and the compact, early 'Little Gem', sweet flavoured but not self folding.

Crispheads include the popular 'Webb's Wonderful'; 'Windermere' for growing outdoors or in a cold frame; and the American-style, white 'Iceberg' for late spring or early summer sowing.

Butterhead varieties include the dwarf 'Tom Thumb'; the bolt-resistant 'All the Year Round'; and 'Avondefiance', the best for summer sowing. Winter-hardy butterheads include 'Valdor', 'Imperial Winter' and 'Arctic King'. For forcing under glass choose 'Dandie', 'Kloek' or 'Kweik'.

# MARROWS AND COURGETTES

Marrow
'Long Green Trailing'

Marrows and courgettes, pumpkins, squashes and cucumbers all belong to the cucurbit family. Though botanically fruits, containing the seeds of future offspring, they are used like vegetables in the kitchen. Marrows and courgettes are easier to grow than cucumbers, and are considered more acceptable at the dining table than pumpkins and squashes, which have slightly eccentric or foreign overtones. Courgettes or zucchini, are immature marrows, although some varieties have been specially developed for harvesting at the courgette stage.

Courgettes are ideal vegetables for the small garden, especially if a bush form is chosen. The plants are attractive in leaf and flower; adequate soil preparation and regular watering are the only real requirements; the ratio of crop to space taken is high; and the crop itself is delicious. Young courgettes can be served raw in salads; lightly cooked and cooled à la grecque; fried, boiled, or grated and made into fritters.

While marrow is equally good in the garden, in the kitchen it has only its size to recommend it. So it acts as a container for mince, onions and tomatoes. Its own flavour is so elusive as to be non-existent, and its traditional use as a filler for chutneys and jams – marrow and ginger, for example – is the best one.

The Italians dip the golden yellow, tubular flowers of courgettes in batter and deep fry them. The flowers can also be served fresh, stuffed with a soft cheese, as an unusual hors d'œuvre, or used as a very pretty garnish.

## Site and soil

Huge trailing marrows were traditionally grown on manure or compost heaps. Such plants produced lush, monstrous foliage and elephantine, tasteless fruit. Rich, moisture-retentive soil is a reasonable alternative, as long as there is sun and shelter.

You are unlikely to want more than a few plants, so prepare individual positions. In early or mid-spring enrich an area 37.5cm (15in) square and deep with well rotted compost, leaving it slightly mounded. Space sites 60-90cm (2-3ft) apart for bush forms, and 1.2-1.5m (4-5ft) apart for trailing ones. The latter can also be trained up wigwams, walls and fences as long as the fruit are not too heavy. A week or so before sowing or planting, rake in a general-purpose fertilizer.

## Cultivation

Since growing marrows and courgettes is a race against frost, many people start the plants under glass in mid-spring for a head start. Sow singly and on edge in 7.5cm (3in) peat pots and provide a temperature of 18°C (65°F); germination takes about a week. Seeds will germinate at 10°C (50°F), but they take twice as long to do so. If the young plants run out of

Marrow
'Long Green Striped'

nutrients, water or root space, they take longer to recover than the time gained from early sowing, so pot on as soon as necessary into 12.5cm (5in) pots of John Innes potting compost No. 2 or 3. Keep well watered and harden off before planting out after the last frost.

Alternatively, in late spring sow two or three seeds on each prepared mound, on edge, 2.5cm (1in) deep and as much apart. Cloche and thin the seedlings to the strongest in each group. Hoe carefully and very shallowly, and water in dry weather. (Marrows growing on compost heaps will need extra watering.) Mulch after watering to conserve soil moisture and discourage weeds. In very hot dry weather mist the leaves to keep down red spider mite. Slug pellets are another sensible precaution.

Carefully cover any roots that appear on the soil surface with a thin layer of compost or soil. For early crops, and in wet, windy or unseasonably cold weather, hand pollination is necessary. Take a male flower, backed by some stalk, turn back its petals and gently dab it into the centre of a female flower, identifiable by a tiny fruit behind it. Once the young fruit swell, feed weekly with dilute liquid fertilizer. Place developing marrows on tiles, panes of glass or shallow wooden boxes to keep them from rotting.

Pinch out the growing tips and the sideshoots of trailing varieties when about 60cm (2ft) long. Allow those trained vertically to reach a suitable height before pinching out.

Marrow
'Green Bush'

(Trailing forms have tendrils and climb naturally.)

In dry conditions the leaves are sometimes covered with a thick white coating of powdery mildew. Remove and burn badly infected leaves, increase watering and spray the plant with fungicide.

## Harvesting and storing

Pick courgettes when 7.5-10cm (3-4in) long; marrows are at their best when 25-30cm (10-12in) long, though those for winter storage should be left on the plant until the first frost threatens. The more you cut, the more flowers and fruit will form.

Courgettes can be blanched and frozen, or kept in a refridgerator for up to a week. Cut marrows for storing with a bit of stalk attached. Store on shelves or hung singly in mesh nets in a cool but frost free, dry place. Never store marrows touching each other.

## Varieties

The dark-green, pale-striped 'Long Green Trailing' and its pale-green-skinned version 'Long White Trailing' are the old-fashioned, mammoth marrows of show-bench proportions. There are several strains of 'Green Bush' marrow, some earlier or more compact than others; they can be grown for courgettes and then, later in the season, for a marrow or two. 'White Bush' marrow has creamy white, medium-sized fruit. 'Zucchini' is the best courgette-type variety; there are also the yellow-skinned 'Golden Zucchini' and the earlier cropping 'Gold Rush'.

Courgette
'Gold Rush'

# MUSHROOMS

Mushroom
Button

Mushroom
Cup

Cultivated mushrooms are a curiosity crop: botanical curiosities, since they are the fruiting bodies of *Agaricus bisporus*; horticultural curiosities in their desire for dimly lit places; and, finally, quite unpredictable as to when they actually appear. Those who pick wild mushrooms, such as chanterelles, ceps and puffballs, know that certain woodlands or fields may yield hundreds of funghi one year and none the next. Folklore ascribes this to their magical properties. The scientific explanation, however, is that funghi need very specific combinations of soil temperature and moisture content, air temperature and humidity, before the spores (microscopic reproductive cells) will germinate to produce thread-like mycelium (germ tubes), which in turn produce the edible fruiting bodies that we eat as mushrooms.

Compared to wild mushrooms, the flavour of cultivated mushrooms is quite bland. If you have a good greengrocer or supermarket there is little difference in culinary terms between freshly bought and freshly grown ones. On the other hand, watching a cultivated mushroom appear and grow as if by magic does give a primordial thrill, now obtainable through modern domestic mushroom-growing kits.

### Site and soil

An occasional field mushroom (A. campestris) may appear on your lawn, but it is not easy to get a cultivated mushroom to grow there. A lightly shaded lawn growing on richly manured soil, such as a former horse, cow or sheep pasture, is ideal. Lawn treated with fungicide or weedkiller is unsuitable.

Ready-spawned mushroom kits are obtainable, with a container, the spawn-impregnated growing medium, a top dressing, or casing, and instructions. They are totally 'clean' and can be used in any warm, shady spot indoors.

Alternatively, you can make your own mushroom compost, but enormous quantities of manure and straw are needed and it is time consuming, risky and very hard work. Some seed catalogues sell compost maker for converting straw into mushroom compost, or you may be able to buy prepared compost from a commercial grower nearby. You need a scrupulously clean, draught-free, waterproof shed or cellar, and deep boxes or buckets to hold the compost. Disinfect containers before use.

Mushroom
Flat

### Cultivation

Mushroom spawn is available as blocks of fungus-impregnated dried manure, or as quicker-growing but riskier fungus-impregnated inert rye grain.

If attempting outdoor cultivation, lift squares of turf on a damp spring or autumn day, water the soil if dry, then crumble block spawn lightly over the soil surface. Replace the turf, firm and water in dry weather. There is nothing else to do. If you are lucky and mushrooms appear, cease mowing until the crop is finished.

The spawn can also be grown indoors on homemade compost. Pack the compost into containers when its temperature is 21°C (70°F); it should be crumbly and sweet smelling. Break block spawn into small pieces and 'plant' it 30cm (12in) apart and 5cm (2in) deep; cover with compost. Alternatively, scatter grain spawn on the surface and cover with black plastic. The temperature of the compost should be 10-18°C (50-65°F) at this stage.

In a week or two, white mycelium threads will appear on the surface of the compost. Cover the surface with a casing 5cm (2in) deep of peat and chalk, mixed three parts to one by volume. Water steadily but moderately; keep the temperature even.

The mushroom kits should be started within three weeks of purchase. Cover the compost with the casing provided, water and keep the temperature between 13-18°C (55-65°F). Follow instructions; water regularly but don't saturate the compost.

**Harvesting and storing**
Cropping may start a month after spawning, but can take up to three months. Mushrooms usually mature in batches, or flushes. Pick by twisting the stem base to break it cleanly; remove any bits of broken stalk from the compost. Fill any holes with more compost and water lightly; a second flush should appear within two weeks. Cropping should continue for two or three months; if it stops before this, water thoroughly to re-activate the growth.

After harvesting is finished, clear out the compost. It is useful in the garden but not for growing mushrooms again. Disinfect containers if using again for another crop. Mushrooms keep refrigerated for a day or two.

**Varieties**
These are not technically varieties, but stages of growth. Button mushrooms, with pure white flesh and hidden gills, are young mushrooms. As they grow the membrane covering the gills breaks; mushrooms at this stage are known as cup mushrooms. Finally, mature mushrooms are open, or flat ones, with their brownish gills fully exposed. They usually take about a week from the button to the flat stage.

# MUSTARD AND CRESS

More a kitchen crop than a garden one, mustard and cress is a classic combination for sandwiches and salads all year round. Children are very fond of growing mustard and cress because it is trouble free, quick and visible. They are less fond, perhaps, of the peppery taste of this sprouting seed double act.

**Site and soil**
There are mustard and cress growing kits for sale, or the sprouts can be grown on sliced raw potatoes or even melon peels. All you really need, though, is a plain seed tray filled with three or four layers of kitchen towel. Alternatively, use soft flannel or a thin layer of peat in the tray.

**Cultivation**
Wash and rinse a small amount of cress seed, then soak overnight in lukewarm water. The next day soak and drain the towel, flannel or peat, so it is damp not sodden. Drain the seeds then scatter evenly over the growing medium. Put in a dark place with a minimum temperature of 10°C (50°F). The mustard seed is then prepared and sown in the same way. Most books advocate sowing it three days later than the cress, but you may find that it keeps pace with the cress and can be sown at the same time. Keep the growing medium damp and once the seeds begin to sprout move to a well lit spot out of direct sunlight.

**Harvesting and storing**
Harvest when about 2.5cm (1in) high, using scissors to cut the stems at the base. 'Crops' are ready a week or so after sowing, longer in winter.

**Varieties**
There are both curly and plain-leaved cresses; white mustard is usually sold for sprouting.

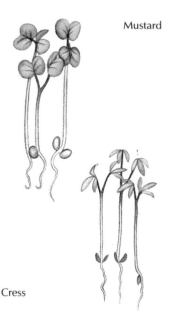

Mustard

Cress

# ONIONS

Few cookery books sing the praises of onions, yet they are an essential ingredient of Mediterranean cuisine, where they were probably first used, and of cookery throughout the world. As well as being the main ingredient of French onion soup and onion tart, they contribute to stews, casseroles, salads, stuffings and sauces.

In the garden, onion is a traditional allotment crop, and growing mammoth prize onions a traditional summer occupation. In very small gardens, spring onions are a better choice; they are quicker growing and take up less space than maincrops, which in any case are cheap all year round.

### Site and soil

Traditionally onions were given the richest soil a garden had to offer and grown in the same spot year after year. While this is less disastrous than growing, say, brassicas in the same spot repeatedly, it is better for the garden as a whole to include onions in a crop rotation system.

Onions like warmth and sunshine, and fertile, light but firm, well drained soil. In the autumn before sowing dig in well rotted compost; if the soil is acid, apply lime in winter. A week before sowing rake in a general-purpose fertilizer. Before sowing, rake the ground roughly level, then tread and rake again for a firm tilth. Grow pickling onions in sandy, poorish soil.

Onion
'White Lisbon'

Onion
'White Spanish'

Onion
'Paris Silverskin'

## Cultivation

There are different types of onions, each with a slightly different method of cultivation. Quick-growing spring onions, or salad onions, are sown from early spring to midsummer for harvesting in summer and autumn; and sown again in late summer for cropping the following spring. Pickling, or button, onions are sown in mid-spring for harvesting in mid- and late summer.

Maincrop onions can either be grown from sets – immature bulbs heat-treated to kill the embryo flower – or from seed. Sets are more expensive, but more tolerant of indifferent soils and growing conditions, and they mature more quickly. They are also more resistant to onion fly and much safer in cold, wet areas and on cold soils. Sets are planted in early or mid-spring for harvesting in late summer.

To grow onions from seed in cold areas, sow under glass in midwinter, harden off in early spring and plant out a month later. Most onions are sown in situ outdoors, in late winter or early spring for harvesting in late summer. Midwinter sowings are possible with cloches. For crops in early or midsummer, sow suitable varieties in late summer to overwinter outdoors.

Space rows for pickling and salad onions 10cm (4in) apart; for the rest, space rows 20-25cm (8-10in) apart. Plant sets and seedlings started under glass 10-15cm (4-6in) apart. The tips of the former should just be visible above the soil surface; the latter should have

Onion
'North Holland Blood Red'

a hole deep enough to take the fully spread out roots, with the bases buried 15mm (½in) below the surface. Firm the soil after planting; later, check that birds have not tweaked out the sets and re-firm if necessary.

Sow Japanese onion seed individually, spaced 2.5cm (1in) apart; thin in spring to 10-15cm (4-6in) apart. Sow spring-sown and salad onions thinly; sow autumn-sown and pickling onions more thickly. Cover with soil and firm.

Thin spring-sown onions to 5cm (2in) apart as soon as possible; thin again to 10-15cm (4-6in) apart. Thin salad, or spring, onions to 2.5cm (1in) apart; pickling onions are not normally thinned. Whenever thinning, water first if the soil is dry, firm the soil round the remaining plants and remove the thinnings to deter onion fly. (Larger thinnings of all types can be used as spring onions.)

Onion leaves are thin and can't compete with weeds. Hoe frequently, carefully and shallowly; hand weed between plants. Water if there is a prolonged dry spell. Mulch to keep weeds down and conserve soil moisture, but don't cover the bulbs.

In top-class soil, onions don't need feeding; otherwise, in early spring feed developing bulbs and autumn-sown plants with a general-purpose fertilizer. Remove any flower stems that appear. Once the bulbs are fully swollen stop watering and draw back the soil to expose and ripen the bulbs. In hot dry summers onion fly maggots burrow into the bases of bulbs, usually those grown from seed. Dust seedlings with calomel as a preventive; lift and burn badly infested plants.

Microscopic eelworm causes distorted foliage and soft, ruined bulbs. Lift and burn infested plants; don't grow onions in the garden for at least two years.

White rot is a self-descriptive fungal infection, most prevalent in hot, dry summers. Lift and burn infected plants; don't grow onions on the same ground for eight years. Calomel dusted onto the seed drills helps prevent the infection.

**Harvesting and storing**
In good weather, when onions are fully grown their foliage turns yellow and bends over naturally, the neck shrinks and ripening begins. In wet weather, the foliage of fully grown bulbs should be bent over by hand to start the process. Leave in situ for two weeks, exposed (hopefully) to the sun, then harvest when the weather is dry, using a fork or pulling by hand.

Japanese onions can't be stored, nor can damaged, diseased, soft, huge, or thick-necked onions. Use immediately, blanch and freeze, give them away or place on the compost heap. (Diseased onions should be burned.) Clean off the soil from bulbs suitable for storing. Dry outdoors in fine weather by placing them in a single layer on sacking, gravel paths, or wire mesh trays. In wet weather place them indoors on wire-mesh racks so the air can

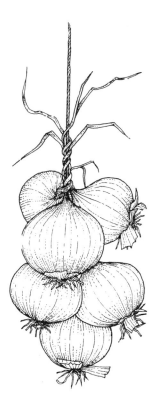

Making an onion rope

circulate freely around them. Drying can take up to three weeks, depending on the weather, the variety and the size of the bulbs; when the foliage is papery and brittle, onions can be stored.

Store in a dry, cool, light, well ventilated spot; properly ripened and dried onions tolerate a few degrees of frost. Make a traditional onion rope by knotting the dried leaves through twine, or store in mesh bags, old nylon tights or in single layers in trays.

Pull spring onions when the bulbs or bases are 15-25mm (½-1in) in diameter; they keep refrigerated for a week. Harvest pickling varieties when 2.5cm (1in) across.

## Varieties

Spring onions include the old-fashioned favourite 'White Lisbon', suitable for spring or late summer sowing, and 'White Lisbon Winter Hardy' for late summer sowing only. The Oriental spring onion 'Ishikura' does not form a bulb, only mild-flavoured leaves.

The most popular pickling onion is 'Paris Silverskin'; others are 'Aviv', formerly called 'Quicksilver', and 'The Queen'.

Not all onion varieties are available as sets. Those that are include the long-keeping, bolt-resistant 'Stuttgarter Giant'; the equally admirable 'Sturon'; 'Rijnsburger' or 'Giant Fen Globe'; and the old favourite, 'Ailsa Craig'.

For maincrops sown in late winter or spring, 'Bedfordshire Champion' is a heavy cropper and good keeper; 'Ailsa Craig' is a good cropper, but poor keeper. The large, flat bulbs of 'White Spanish' do keep well, and so does the attractively red-skinned 'North Holland Blood Red'.

Good late summer and early autumn-sown varieties include 'Autumn Queen'; 'Buffalo' (an $F_1$ hybrid also suitable for spring sowing) and 'Reliance'. Japanese varieties for autumn sowing include 'Express Yellow', early, but with only moderate yields; and the similar 'Extra Early Kaizuka'.

# PARSNIPS

Parsnip is easy to grow, but takes a lot of time and space and is not the best choice for tiny gardens.

## Site and soil
Choose sun or light shade, and a firm, fertile, well drained soil, not too acid. Ideally, the soil should have been enriched for a previous crop, since stony or freshly enriched soil leads to forked roots. Lime, if necessary, in winter and rake in a general-purpose fertilizer a week before sowing.

Parsnip
'Avonresister'

## Cultivation
Sow seed in situ in late winter or early spring. Make the drills 15mm (½in) deep and 30cm (12in) apart. Sow two or three seeds every 15cm (6in), then cover with soil, firm and water if necessary. Germination can take a month, but a quick-growing catch crop such as radish can be sown along the rows to mark them and make maximum use of space. When the parsnip seedlings appear, thin to one per station.

Water only in dry weather and keep weeds down. Try not to damage the roots with the hoe, as the fungal infection canker can attack the root where it is damaged. Since there is no cure, good cultivation is the best prevention. Aphids attack the leaves in hot, dry summers; hand pick the worst leaves and spray the rest with an insecticide suitable for crops. (See also Carrots for carrot fly.)

## Harvesting and storing
Begin harvesting in autumn when the leaves die down, and continue lifting roots as needed until late winter when the remaining crop should be cleared. Alternatively, lift and store in boxes of peat or sand before the ground freezes.

## Varieties
Long varieties such as 'Tender and True' are best for exhibiting, but for ordinary use, a short-rooted variety such as 'Avonresister' is better.

# PEAS

Peas

Fresh peas are one of the finest rewards of vegetable growing, and picking and shelling peas, provided the weather is fine and the pace leisurely, is as enjoyable as eating them. In spite of the advertising claims of the pea processors, fresh peas *are* nicer than frozen or canned ones. In fact, the sugar content of peas changes to starch soon after picking and the flavour diminishes accordingly, so home-grown peas, cooked within a few minutes of picking, are nicest of all.

So why doesn't everyone grow peas? They take up a lot of space in proportion to the size of the crop; they don't like hot weather and most types stop forming pods above 20°C (70°F); they don't like frost and they don't like drought. Also, they are not tolerant of indifferent soils and are much sought after by birds, mice and a host of other garden pests. One either grows peas with whole-hearted committment or not at all.

In the kitchen, peas are good lightly boiled or steamed, and flavoured with mint and butter in the English fashion. Peas *à la française*, with lettuce, shallots, butter and a touch of sugar, are also delicious. Young peas can be served raw in salads; very old peas can be puréed and sieved, though allowing garden peas to reach this state is rather a waste. Cottagers made pea-pod wine, and blenders (combined with

Pea
'Feltham First'

sieves) make pea-pod soup possible. Mangetout, a variety of pea picked when immature and eaten whole and the tiny, sweet-flavoured dwarf-growing petit pois are both considered supreme delicacies. Both can be eaten raw or lightly cooked. For those who don't mind the fiddly preparation, fresh mangetout can be carefully slit open and piped with a soft, savoury filling.

**Site and soil**
The best soil is heavy, neutral, warm and rich, but not recently enriched. Peas, like other legumes, can extract nitrogen from the air, and excessive nitrates in the soil result in lush, weak growth and few pods. The soil should also be moisture retentive but well drained, and deep enough to accommodate the long roots. Dig over the soil in the autumn before sowing, incorporating well rotted compost. Lime, if necessary, in winter, and rake in a little general-purpose fertilizer a week before sowing.

A sunny, open site is best; shelter is essential for early crops and tall-growing forms. The latter will shade nearby crops, but in high summer this shade is useful for lettuce, radish, spinach and carrots.

**Cultivation**
There are several types of peas, each with slightly different requirements. As well as tall-growing peas, there are dwarf forms. According to the length of time from sowing to harvesting, which is usually from eleven to fourteen weeks, peas are divided into first

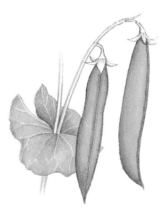
Pea
'Kelvedon Wonder'

Pea
'Oregon Sugar Pod'

earlies, second earlies and maincrops. Round-seeded peas are first earlies, usually dwarf, hardier and generally more tolerant than wrinkle-seeded varieties. The latter are better flavoured and heavier cropping, but are less hardy. There are first early, second early and maincrop varieties of wrinkle-seeded peas; and dwarf and tall-growing forms.

Some people sow round-seeded peas in mid- or late autumn. Given a mild winter and cloche protection, they mature a couple of weeks earlier than spring-sown ones. In a bad winter there is no advantage, and the crop may even be lost. It is safer to start under cloches in late winter or early spring, for late spring and early summer crops. Sow in early or mid-spring for midsummer crops, using round, first early or second-early wrinkled varieties. Sow maincrops, mangetout and petit pois in mid- or late spring for late summer crops. For a final autumn crop, sow first earlies in early or midsummer.

Sow peas in situ, in drills 5cm (2in) deep and 15-20cm (6-8in) wide. (If possible, buy seed treated with fungicide.) Make the distance between the drills equal to the expected height of the plants. Space seeds 5-7.5cm (2-3in) apart, closer for autumn sowings which tend to suffer more mortalities. Cover and firm.

Protect from birds at once with wire-mesh pea guards, criss-crossed black cotton, or brushwood laid on the soil surface. Once seedlings appear hoe between rows and hand weed between plants. Water in dry weather, and mulch with well rotted compost to retain soil moisture and discourage weeds.

All peas, even dwarf forms, need support and their tendrils cling naturally; twiggy hazel sticks are traditional, with taller sticks along the outside of the rows and broken off, and smaller twiggy sticks pushed in near their base to help the young plants gain a foothold. Birch or chestnut branches can also be used. For tall varieties, use wire mesh or plastic netting along each side of the row, stretched between two poles. Provide support when the plants are 7.5-10cm (3-4in) high; left trailing on the ground, they are vulnerable to slugs and the stems become kinked. Make the supports 15cm (6in) higher than the height of the plants. If birds attack developing pods (they are particularly fond of mangetout), drape fine mesh netting over the supports as protection.

Maggots of the pea moth tunnel into the seed; as a preventive, spray thoroughly with fenitrothion a week after flowering starts. Pea thrips cause distorted pods (silvery patches, later turning brown, are the first symptoms) and pea weevil eats notches along the leaf edges; in both cases, spray with fenitrothion at the first sign of infestation.

Powdery mildew is a problem in dry weather. Burn badly infected plants; spray the rest with benomyl or dinocap.

After harvesting leave the nitrogen-rich roots in the soil. If

Pea
'Purple Podded'

the plants are pest and disease free, put the top growth on the compost heap, if not burn it.

## Harvesting and storing

Pick mangetout before the peas begin swelling. Pick other peas when the pod is filled but not fully mature; the peas inside should almost touch each other. The more peas are picked, the more are produced. Never leave old pods hanging on the plant as they inhibit further production. Pick from the bottom of the plant upwards, either using scissors or by hand, supporting the stem with one hand.

Peas can be blanched and frozen and will keep for three or four days refrigerated. Peas left to mature fully on the plant can be dried; in wet weather bring the plants indoors and hang upside down in a well ventilated, dry spot.

## Varieties

There are dozens of varieties of peas and the following is a reasonable selection. The earliest round-seeded pea is 'Feltham First', 45cm (18in) high. 'Pilot', at 90cm (3ft) high, is a heavy cropping round-seeded form and 'Meteor' is a dwarf form 30cm (12in) high, reputedly extra hardy. Of the wrinkle-seeded varieties, first earlies include the popular 'Kelvedon Wonder', the very early 'Progress No. 9' and 'Little Marvel', all at 45cm (18in).

Second early wrinkle-seeded varieties include the all-time favourite 'Onward' and the reliable and disease-resistant 'Hurst Green Shaft' both at 75cm (2½ft). Taller growing, and particularly good for freezing is 'Miracle'. Maincrops include the 1.5m (5ft) high 'Alderman' with large pods and high yields; the late-maturing 'Lord Chancellor' at 90cm (3ft); and the compact-growing 'Senator' at 75cm (2½ft).

Petit pois varieties include 'Cobri' and 'Waverex', both 60cm (2ft) high. 'Oregon Sugar Pod', 1.2m (4ft) high, and the slighly shorter 'Sugar Dwarf Sweet Green' are mangetout varieties. The 1.5m (5ft) high 'Sugar Snap' has pods that can be treated as mangetout when immature; when mature, they can be shelled and treated as 'proper' peas.

# PEPPERS AND CHILLIS

Sweet peppers, capsicums and bell peppers are one and the same: the familiar vegetable used raw in salads or Spanish gazpacho, cooked in ratatouille, or stuffed and baked. Green peppers are unripe; red and yellow ones, according to variety, are the same fruit but fully ripe. Peppers are delicious either way, a fortunate state of affairs since in cool temperate climates they don't often ripen fully before the first autumn frost. For this reason, peppers and chillis, their fiercely flavoured cousins, are best grown as greenhouse crops, though you can try growing peppers outdoors.

### Site and soil
If cultivating peppers and chillis outdoors, choose a sunny, sheltered spot at the base of a south-facing wall. Enrich the soil the autumn before planting; a week before planting, rake in a general-purpose fertilizer.

Otherwise, grow peppers and chillis in a cool greenhouse, singly in 22.5cm (9in) pots or two or three plants per grow bag. They can also be grown in an open greenhouse border, with soil prepared as for outdoors.

### Cultivation
Start all peppers and chillis under glass, in late winter for a greenhouse crop and in early spring for an outdoor one. Sow thinly in trays of seed compost

Chillis

137

or sow two seeds per peat pot. Provide a minimum temperature of 18°C (65°F). Germination can take up to three weeks. As soon as the seedlings are large enough to handle, either prick out into 7.5cm (3in) pots filled with John Innes potting compost No. 2, or, for those growing in peat pots, thin to the strongest seedling per pot.

Never let peppers or chillis run out of water, nutrients or root space. Water regularly, and pot on young plants before their roots become crowded, first into 12.5cm (5in) pots and, ultimately (if not planted in the open ground or grow bags) into 22.5 cm (9in) pots filled with John Innes potting compost No. 3.

In mid-spring, begin hardening off those plants for planting outdoors after the last frost. Use cloches to warm up the soil for a week or so beforehand. Space the plants 45cm (18in) apart, in rows 45cm (18in) apart. Water thoroughly, then return the cloches to continue protecting the young plants, until they outgrow the cloches.

Peppers and chillis like high humidity and high temperatures, not only because their leaves are thin and wilt easily, but because the humidity helps keep red spider mite from becoming a major problem. Spray the plants daily, but avoid leaving pools of water on the greenhouse floor since this encourages botrytis.

Spraying the plants when the flowers are open also assists pollination. When nine or ten fruit have set (peppers are

Pepper
'Gypsy'

botanically fruit) pinch off any further flowers that form. Chillis can carry heavier crops so no restrictions are needed. Once pepper and chilli fruit start to swell, feed weekly with a liquid fertilizer, such as that used for tomatoes.

Large plants may need staking. Though peppers growing outdoors need all the sunshine they can get, those in greenhouses may need shading during the hottest part of the day in summer.

**Harvesting and storing**
Using a sharp knife, harvest peppers and chillis when full size, which varies according to variety. Pick either ripe or unripe as wished, though obviously at the end of the season all unripe fruit should be harvested. Wear gloves whenever handling chillis, in the garden or kitchen, as they can cause skin irritation. Chillis and peppers will keep for up to two weeks refrigerated. Traditionally, chillis are pickled in vinegar or threaded together in long 'necklaces' to dry in a sunny window.

**Varieties**
Use $F_1$ hybrids, such as 'Canape', 'New Ace' or 'Gypsy'; 'Canape' is the least risky for growing outdoors. The chilli 'Cayenne Pepper' is reliable for greenhouse cropping.

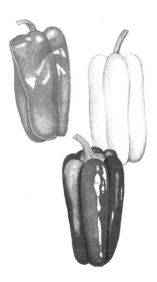

Peppers

# POTATOES

Potatoes have come a long way since they were introduced to Europe from South America in the sixteenth century. Originally grown only as cattle food by Europeans, the potato was subject to various prejudices; some people, for example, refused to eat potatoes because there was no mention of them in the Bible. Gradually their value was recognized, and today potatoes are an accepted part of the daily diet.

Like other 'dual-personality' vegetables, such as carrots, turnips and beetroot, new or early potatoes are totally different from their matured, stored winter counterparts. The first new potatoes of early summer are the vegetable equivalent of the first *Beaujolais Nouveau* of autumn.

Those with small gardens should grow only new potatoes. Maincrop potatoes, though giving heavier crops, take up a great deal of space, and stored maincrops taste much the same whether from one's own garden or from a shop. New potatoes are relatively expensive to buy, and the range of those commercially available is restricted to those that travel and keep well. These are two good reasons to grow your own; the third is the pleasure derived from digging them up: an edible treasure hunt for the 'fruits' – or more correctly the tubers – of your labour.

Potatoes

### Site and soil

Potatoes are tolerant of a wide range of soil types, but one potato crop should never follow another. The ideal soil is deep, friable, and neutral or slightly acid; various scab infections are encouraged by the presence of lime. Traditionally, potatoes were the first crop grown on ground newly converted from pasture. This doesn't mean that potatoes do well in poor, starved soil; such pastures often contained decades of manure. Fresh compost or manure however is unsuitable, as is fertilizer rich in nitrates; these result in lush top growth, or haulm, and poor crops.

If the soil was not enriched for a previous crop, work in well rotted compost the autumn before planting. A week before planting, apply a general-purpose fertilizer.

Though potatoes are frost-tender, they don't really like baking heat. Full sun, but cool, moist conditions are ideal. Avoid low-lying or exposed ground and frost pockets, especially for early crops.

Seed potatoes sprouting in an egg box

### Cultivation

Though plant breeders work with the seed produced by the small, white flowers, crops are always grown from dormant tubers, variously known as sets, seed or seed potatoes. *Always* buy certified, virus-free seed potatoes; the best size is that of a hen's egg.

For early crops, seed potatoes are chitted, or started into growth before being planted. Though not necessary for maincrops, chitting does give the plants a head start and generally results in heavier yields. In late winter, place the potatoes rose-end up in egg boxes, or tightly butted up in a single layer in shallow trays. The rose end is where the 'eyes', or incipient growth buds, are clustered. Place the potatoes in a cool but frost-free spot, well lit but not in direct sunlight. In four to six weeks, when the pale sprouts are 15-25mm ($\frac{1}{2}$-1in) long the potatoes are ready for planting.

Like peas, there are early, second early and maincrop potatoes, depending on the length of time from sowing to harvesting. Plant first earlies in early spring for harvesting in early or midsummer. Plant second earlies in mid-spring for harvesting in mid- and late summer. Plant maincrops in mid- or late spring for lifting in late summer and early autumn.

Using a draw hoe, make drills 10-15cm (4-6in) deep; the heavier the soil, the shallower the drill. Space the rows 45-60cm (18-24in) apart for earlies, and 75cm (2$\frac{1}{2}$ft) apart for maincrops. Seed potatoes are sometimes planted in individual holes using a dibber or trowel, but this is risky because any air-pocket left beneath the tuber will fill with water and cause rotting. Scattering grass cuttings in the drill before planting helps prevent scab. Place the chitted potatoes suitably spaced out and sprout-end up. Carefully cover the sprouts by hand with fine crumbly soil or a bit of peat, then fill in the drills and finish with a low ridge.

Potato
'Duke of York'

Potato
'Desiree'

Potato
'Pentland Crown'

# POTATOES

Frost can blacken young shoots but this is rarely fatal, though several weeks' growth can be lost. Cover small shoots with soil if frost threatens. Protect taller growth with upturned flower pots, jars, a layer of straw or bracken, or cloches. Water in dry weather to prevent split or hollow tubers. Hoe to keep weeds down and the soil surface open, but be careful of damaging the stems.

Earth up when the haulms are 20-22.5cm (8-9in) high. Fork over the soil between the rows; then, using a draw hoe, mound it loosely around the stems to form a flat-topped ridge 15cm (6in) high. This can be done in one go, or in several stages. Earthing up is necessary to keep the tubers protected from sunlight, otherwise they turn green and become inedible. An alternative is to grow potatoes on the flat, using sheets of black polythene, tucked into the soil, over the rows. Immediately after planting, water thoroughly and scatter slug pellets over the ground, then cover with polythene. Slit the polythene above the young growth once it begins pushing against the polythene.

The worst problems – the self-descriptive leaf roll virus and mosaic viruses (usually seen as yellow-mottled leaves) – are prevented by buying virus-free seed and controlling aphids, which transmit virus. The fungal infection blight can destroy entire crops; maincrops in wet weather are most vulnerable. Symptoms are browny black patches on the leaves. Spray with

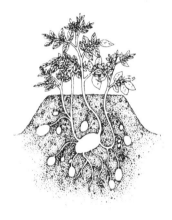

Section through an earthed-up potato plant

Bordeaux mixture in mid- and late summer, and burn badly infected foliage.

Capsid bugs eat holes in the leaves and cause stunted growth; spray with fenitrothion at the first sign of infestation.

**Harvesting and storing**
Begin checking first and second earlies once the flowers open; the immature tubers are ready for lifting when the size of a hen's egg, or slightly smaller. Insert a fork (ideally, a flat-tined potato fork) at an angle into the soil, well away from the stems. For the best flavour, cook earlies as soon as possible after lifting, though they will keep refrigerated for ten days or two weeks.

Maincrops start maturing when the haulm yellows and shrivels. A week or two later, lift the crop and leave it on the soil surface for an hour or so to dry, then prepare for storage. Clean off the soil adhering to the tubers and inspect them. Store only those that are free of pests, diseases and damage; in short, free of suspicion. Don't store tubers with skins that can be rubbed off. Use wooden boxes or brown paper bags for storage; keep in a cool but frost-free, dry dark place, and inspect monthly. (An old-fashioned alternative is to build a clamp in the garden but few people bother nowadays.)

When harvesting, try to clear the soil of all tubers; those that remain are a nuisance and can harbour pests and diseases.

**Varieties**
Certain varieties do best in certain soil types, weather conditions and localities. The following is a general guide; before choosing, check with your local garden centre. Tried and true first earlies include the kidney-shaped 'Duke of York'; the oval, waxy-fleshed 'Pentland Javelin'; the oval 'Sutton's Foremost' and the round 'Epicure'.

Second earlies include the oval, yellow-fleshed 'Estima'; the oval, white-fleshed 'Red Craig's Royal' and the old-fashioned, round 'Great Scot', ideal for baking.

Maincrops include 'Desiree', oval waxy and yellow fleshed; 'Maris Piper', a high yielding, good tasting pale-fleshed form; and 'Pentland Crown', a heavy cropping, white-fleshed oval form.

# PUMPKINS AND SQUASHES

Squash
'Hubbard'

With pumpkins, the lure of the enormous reaches its zenith. Whether for harvest festivals, exhibitions or local competitions, the prospect of growing hundredweight pumpkins has captivated thousands of gardeners. Both pumpkins and squashes are closely related to marrows and courgettes, and are grown in much the same way, but squashes are smaller scale and range in shape, colour, size and taste.

In the kitchen, the firm, tasty yellow-orange flesh of pumpkins and winter squashes is used, American fashion, in pumpkin pie, cream of pumpkin soup and pumpkin pudding; it is also good sliced and roast around a joint. The hollowed out pumpkin shell is the Hallowe'en jack-o-lantern, and dried, fried and salted pumpkin seeds are a traditional snack.

The soft flesh of summer squash is usually baked, boiled or braised, and needs plenty of seasoning to overcome its bland taste.

### Site and soil

Pumpkins and squashes can be grown on compost heaps, and in America a few pumpkin plants are often grown between rows of sweetcorn. Pumpkins and squashes are greedy feeders, needing rich, moisture retentive but not waterlogged soil, and full sun. A single pumpkin plant, or a couple of squashes, is as much as most

Pumpkin 'Mammoth'

small gardens can readily accommodate, so prepare the ground accordingly. For each plant, in the spring before sowing or planting, enrich an area 37.5cm (15in) square and deep with well rotted compost. Leave it slightly mounded to throw water away from the stems, which are very vulnerable to grey mould if wet. Space plants 90cm (3ft) apart if growing more than one. A week or so before sowing or planting, work in a general-purpose fertilizer.

**Cultivation**
Squashes and pumpkins are half-hardy so in cool temperate climates most catalogues advocate sowing indoors in early spring. Sow seeds on edge and singly in 7.5cm (3in) peat pots and provide a temperature of 21°C (70°F). Germination takes about a week. Plants grow quickly and should be potted on, before they become root-bound, into 12.5cm (5in) pots filled with John Innes potting compost No. 2 or 3. Keep well watered, then harden off and plant out when the danger of frost is over. Be prepared to cloche or otherwise protect young plants at night and if the weather turns cold.

Alternatively, in late spring sow two or three seeds, 2.5cm (1in) deep, on each mound. Cloche and, when the seedlings appear, remove all but the strongest in each group. This is risky in terms of weather, and the growing season is shorter, but the bother and risk of transplanting is eliminated.

Squash
'Custard Yellow'

Water the plants steadily and generously, avoid wetting the foliage or stems. Hand weed or hoe, but try not to damage the shallow roots. Mulch with well rotted compost to discourage weeds and retain soil moisture. Scatter slug pellets around the plants.

Left alone, pumpkins and trailing squashes can take over a garden, making 5m (16ft) of leafy growth. Pinch out the growing tips of main and side shoots when the stems are about 60cm (2ft) long. Bush squashes are self controlled and need no pinching out.

To ensure cropping, hand fertilize: pick off a male flower, which is attached to a thin stalk, push back the petals, and dab the centre into the centre of a female flower, which has a tiny fruit behind it. Allow only two or three pumpkins per plant – one if you are going for giantism – and remove any others that form. Squashes can produce at will.

When the fruit begin to swell, feed weekly with dilute liquid fertilizer. Place a tile, pane of glass or shallow wooden box under each fruit to keep it from coming into contact with the soil which may cause it to rot.

Pests and diseases are those that afflict marrows and courgettes (see page 121).

**Harvesting and storing**

Harvest summer squashes as soon as fully grown, according to variety. These will keep refrigerated for up to a week. Leave winter squashes and pumpkins on the vine until the first frost threatens, then cut cleanly with a sharp knife, leaving 5-7.5cm (2-3in) of stem attached. These can be kept for months in a cool place, provided they are not touching one another and are inspected regularly.

**Varieties**

'Mammoth' and 'Hundredweight' are the traditional pumpkins; both are trailing. Winter squashes include the old-fashioned, trailing 'Hubbard' and the $F_1$ hybrid bush form 'Table Ace'. All of these need hot, sunny summers to do well.

Summer squashes include the trailing, melon-shaped 'Vegetable Spaghetti', whose flesh, when boiled, is like spaghetti – in texture if not in flavour – and the flat, scallop-shaped 'Custard Yellow'. There is also a similar 'Custard White'.

# RADISHES

Growing radish is child's play for adults as well as children. It is one of the easiest vegetables to cultivate, and one of the quickest, reaching maturity before short attention spans wander.

As well as the universally popular, sweet-fleshed, round summer radishes, there are intermediate or cylindrical ones, yellow-skinned ones and long white peppery ones. Less well known are winter radishes, larger and coarser flavoured but useful raw in winter salads or cooked like turnips. Radish seed can be germinated in a jar, like bean sprouts, and its peppery shoots added to salads or sandwiches.

In the garden, radish is a hard-working vegetable. Because it germinates in less than a week, radish is often mixed with slower growing vegetable seeds, such as carrot or onion, to mark the rows and space out the seedlings of the more permanent crop. Radish is also an ideal catch crop, ready for lifting as little as three weeks after sowing.

In the kitchen, radishes have a distinctly limited role and they rarely appear in cookery books. Though the radish rose has become the caterers' standard symbol of elegant dining, and paper-thin radish slices are *de rigueur* in fast-food salads, radishes are nicest served whole, scrubbed and with a stump of foliage left on as a handle. Accompanying drinks, or as part of a simple

Radish
'French Breakfast'

Radish
'Cherry Belle'

Radish
'Long White Icicle'

hors-d'œuvre, radishes are at their honest best.

**Site and soil**
Although the ideal soil is sandy, well drained but moisture retentive, and fertile but not recently enriched, radishes tolerate other soils as long as they are not waterlogged. If the soil was not enriched for a previous crop, work in well rotted compost in the autumn before sowing. While small summer radishes penetrate only the top few centimetres (or inch) of soil, long white summer radishes and winter ones need a good depth of fine, stone-free soil if they are not to become mis-shapen. A week or so before sowing, rake in a general-purpose fertilizer.

Early and late sowings of summer and winter radishes need full sun and shelter. Summer radish sown from late spring onwards needs dappled shade, conveniently provided by beans, peas or other tall vegetables, to discourage bolting.

**Cultivation**
Traditionally, the first radish crops were sown in early winter, in cold frames on hot beds made of fermenting manure. You can sow summer varieties suitable for forcing in mid- or late winter, in the border of a cool greenhouse, in cold frames, or under cloches. (Rows of radishes fit neatly under cloches with rows of early lettuce.) Put cloches in position a week or two beforehand to warm up the soil first. Sow small amounts of

Radish
'China Rose'

summer radish outdoors, in the open, every two weeks from early spring to early summer; after that, the risk of bolting increases.

Make one sowing of winter radish in mid- or late summer for harvesting from mid-autumn onwards.

Make the drills 15mm (½in) deep and 15cm (6in) apart for summer varieties, 25cm (10in) apart for winter ones. Radish seed is large enough to be station sown; sow thinly, spacing the seed about 2.5cm (1in) apart, then cover with soil and firm. As soon as the seedlings appear, thin larger types of summer radish to 5cm (2in) apart, long white radishes to 10cm (4in) apart, and winter radishes to 15cm (6in) apart. (Overcrowded conditions result in leaf, rather than root, growth.)

Some people sow radish broadcast, scattering seed on a prepared patch of ground. Though a seductive idea, there are difficulties. Hand weeding is necessary, and more thinning than for those sown in drills; this, because radish doesn't transplant well, entails more waste.

The seeds and young plants of radish are attractive to birds, so protect the crop, if not already cloched, with wire-mesh netting or criss-crossed black cotton.

Water steadily, especially in dry weather, so there is no check to growth. Hoe between rows to keep weeds down; hand weed, if necessary, between plants.

Although radishes are, on the whole, pest and disease

free, flea beetle can be troublesome. If holes appear in the foliage of seedlings and young leaves, and if the older leaves are skeletonized, treat with derris. Radish is a member of the brassica family, and as such is occasionally vulnerable to club root. (See Brussels Sprouts, page 68.)

**Harvesting and storing**

With one or two exceptions (see below) summer radishes left to mature and form flower stems will become hollow, woody and unpleasant tasting. The optimum size for picking depends on variety, but generally round types should be 20-25mm (¾-1in) in

Radish
'Black Spanish Round'

diameter; intermediate types 5-7.5cm (2-3in) long; and long white radishes 15-30cm (6-12in) long.

Radishes keep refrigerated for a week, but don't freeze well. If, through miscalculation you have more radishes than you can eat, give them away or put them on the compost heap.

In mild areas, winter radish can be left in the ground and pulled as needed, as it does not degenerate once mature. Protect from frost with a layer of straw. Alternatively, lift the crop in mid-autumn, and store in boxes of sand or peat in a cool but frost-free place.

**Varieties**

Popular summer varieties include the round 'Cherry Belle' and 'Red Prince', both of which can be safely left in the ground for a little while without risk of bolting. 'Robino' and 'Saxerre' are round, red, summer varieties recommended for early sowing under glass or cloches. Intermediate summer varieties include the ever-popular red-and-white 'French Breakfast', and the unusual, yellow-skinned 'Yellow Gold'. There are also mixed packets of popular summer varieties available. Long white radishes include the standard 'Long White Icicle' and the Japanese-type 'Minowase Summer' $F_1$ hybrid. Winter radishes include the self-descriptive 'Black Spanish Round'; the cylindrical, red-skinned 'China Rose', and the mild-flavoured, long, thin 'Mino Early'. All have white flesh and should be peeled before use.

# RHUBARB

Rhubarb
'Champagne Early'

Rhubarb is a long-lived, ultra-hardy Siberian perennial with a very modest following. Technically a vegetable, rhubarb is used like a fruit to make various crumbles, pies and jams when other, more popular fruit is out of season or expensive. Stewed rhubarb with custard is notorious, and rhubarb rarely features on gourmet menus or in gourmet cookery books. Still, it is an undemanding plant with a statuesque presence in the garden: its stalks can be had from midwinter, from forced plants, to midsummer from open-grown late varieties. The leaves contain oxalic acid and should not be eaten.

### Site and soil
Rhubarb will tolerate any soil that is not waterlogged, but grows best in deep, rich, slightly acid soil in full sun. Shelter from strong winds is necessary; low-lying frost pockets are unsuitable.

Dig the ground deeply — 60cm (2ft) is not excessive — in autumn and incorporate a generous amount of well rotted compost. If growing more than one plant, space them 90cm (3ft) apart. Remove every trace of perennial weed at the same time. A week or so before planting, rake in a general-purpose fertilizer.

### Cultivation
Theoretically, young plants can be grown from seed. Realistically, cropping is

**Rhubarb**
**Forced stalks**

delayed, the quality of seedlings varies enormously and few gardens have enough room to grow rhubarb on a scale to justify this economy.

Some seed catalogues and garden centres sell young plants in 7.5cm (3in) or 12.5cm (5in) pots; others sell dormant 'sets' in the form of fang-like roots with one or two growth buds or 'eyes'. Plants and sets should be planted in early spring with the growth buds just showing above the surface of the soil. Firm, water if the soil is dry, and surround with a mulch of well rotted compost or leafmould.

Keep weeds down until the huge leaves do the job themselves; water in dry weather. Remove any flower heads that start to form, breaking them off at the base. Feed the plants with dilute liquid fertilizer after harvesting, and with a mulch of well rotted compost in mid- or late winter. Lift and divide old, weakened plants in spring, every five to ten years, replanting the outer, younger sets in a fresh spot in the garden, and discarding the central, older portion.

Honey fungus, the dreaded enemy of trees, shrubs and thick-rooted perennials, sometimes attacks rhubarb. Infected plants wilt and die; their roots may have thin, white, thread-like strands, or thicker, black, 'bootlace' growths clinging to them. Dig up and burn infected plants; treating the soil with a fungicide sometimes helps, too. Plant fresh rhubarb elsewhere in the garden. Crown rot is another fungal infection, in which the crown rots away. Treatment is the same as for honey fungus.

Use strong-growing crowns, at least three years old, for forcing. There are several methods, of which the easiest is to cover the crowns with a layer of straw in midwinter, but this gives cropping only two or three weeks earlier than normal. If you cover the crowns with a 60cm (2ft) high, or higher, container – a box, upturned bucket, barrel or tub – which is in turn surrounded with a layer of straw, the process is quicker. (Traditionally fermenting manure was packed round terracotta rhubarb pots to provide heat as well as insulation.)

For very early crops, lift the roots in late autumn, leave them exposed to the elements for a week or so, then plant, tightly together and right-way-up, in boxes filled with damp peat. Keep in a cool, dark shed or cellar, or under blacked-out greenhouse staging. Provide a temperature of 10°C (50°F) and keep watered.

## Harvesting and storing

In the second growing season (the third for plants grown from seed), begin harvesting sparingly in mid-spring. Twist and pull the leaf stalks from the base. When fully established, harvest over a three month period, always leaving four or five stalks to grow on. Stop in midsummer so the plants can build up strength.

Lightly forced crops outdoors are ready in early spring; such plants can be forced only one year in three. Hard-forced rhubarb indoors is ready from midwinter; after forcing, discard the worn-out roots. Rhubarb can be refrigerated or frozen.

## Varieties

'Timperley Early' and 'Hawke's Champagne', sometimes sold as 'Champagne Early', are both reliable. The former is particularly good for forcing; the latter is popular for its deep red colouring and heavy crops. 'The Sutton' is bolt-resistant, with particularly large stalks, and 'Victoria' is a late but heavy cropper.

# SALSIFY AND SCORZONERA

Salsify and scorzonera sound like minor characters from a Gilbert and Sullivan operetta. In fact, they are both long slender root vegetables, members of the daisy family, *Compositae*. Though of unpromising appearance – salsify is dirty white, scorzonera is black – they are delicately flavoured, similar to oyster in the case of salsify, and a sweeter version of parsnip in the case of scorzonera.

Traditionally, the roots are scrubbed, boiled in water containing a few drops of lemon juice, then sliced, peeled and served with melted butter. They can also be fried in batter. Both are easy, but slow-growing crops, best foregone in very small gardens.

### Site and soil
Choose a spot in sun or light shade, and a soil that is fertile, well drained and deep (the roots can be up to 45cm (18in) long). Avoid thin, gravelly or stony soils, and those that have recently been enriched; in these conditions, roots will fork. If the soil is very acid, apply lime in winter, and a week before sowing, rake in a general-purpose fertilizer.

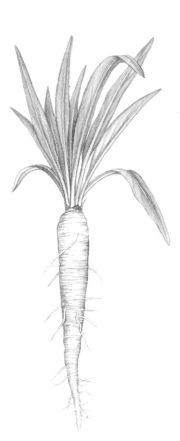

Salsify
'Mammoth Sandwich Island'

### Cultivation
Sow seed, where it is to grow, in mid- or late spring. Make the drills 15mm (½in) deep and 30cm (12in) apart, and sow the seed in clusters of two or three, spaced 20cm (8in) apart. Cover with soil and firm; seedlings

Scorzonera
'Russian Giant'

should appear within two weeks. As soon as they are large enough, thin to the strongest seedling in each group.

Water in dry weather to prevent the plants bolting and, possibly, the roots splitting. Keep weed free, but avoid damaging the roots with a hoe; hand weeding between plants is safest. Mulching with leafmould or well rotted compost in summer helps retain soil moisture and keep weeds down.

The only likely problem is the fungal infection, white blister, which disfigures the foliage and can cause stunted roots. Pick off and burn any infected leaves. There is no cure; good cultivation is the best preventive measure.

**Harvesting and storing**
Harvest from mid-autumn onwards as needed. Be careful not to damage the roots, which 'bleed' if pierced. Break up the soil around the roots, then lever them up, using a fork. Alternatively, lift the whole crop in mid-autumn and store in boxes of sand or peat, in a cool but frost-free place. Roots left in the ground after the end of winter will produce tender spring shoots. The Victorians blanched these shoots, then cooked and served them like asparagus.

Salsify and scorzonera keeps refrigerated for about a week.

**Varieties**
'Russian Giant' is the only scorzonera variety on offer. 'Mammoth Sandwich Island' and 'Giant' are equally acceptable varieties of salsify.

# SEAKALE

Seakale
'Lily White'

Seakale is an eccentric's vegetable, much more popular in Victorian times, when it was a standard winter and spring crop, than today. Like rhubarb, it is a long-term resident of the vegetable garden and, like rhubarb, seakale is grown for its blanched or forced shoots. These are traditionally steamed and served with melted butter like asparagus.

## Site and soil
Seakale grows wild, as its name suggests, by the sea, so sandy, well drained soil and full sun are best. As its name also suggests, it is a member of the brassica family and needs a lime-rich soil with well rotted compost worked in the autumn before planting. A week or so before planting, rake in general-purpose fertilizer.

## Cultivation
Theoretically, seakale can be grown from seed, but it is safer to obtain crowns or cuttings of dormant roots from a friend or an old-fashioned nursery.

Plant in mid-spring, first removing all but one growth bud from each crown. Space them 60cm (2ft) apart in each direction and cover with 5cm (2in) of soil. Keep weeded and well watered, especially in dry weather, and feed occasionally during the growing season with liquid fertilizer. Remove any flower stems that appear. In autumn, cut down the dying foliage, and in early winter begin blanching. You can

Seakale
Blanched stalks

simply cover the dormant crowns with a 15cm (6in) layer of soil or leafmould, but this encourages slugs. A better method of excluding light is to cover the plants with upturned wooden boxes, barrels, buckets or flower pots. (Old-fashioned, lidded, terracotta seakale pots are beautiful but hard to find.) Pile compost or leafmould over and around the container to insulate it; traditionally, a layer of manure was used to provide heat.

For even more work, earlier crops can be obtained. Lift dormant crowns in late autumn, leave them exposed on the ground for a week or so, then trim to 15cm (6in) and pack vertically into pots or boxes of leafmould or peat. The crowns should just be visible. Water lightly, keep dark and maintain a minimum temperature of 7°C (45°F).

## Harvesting and storing
Shoots 20cm (8in) high are ready for harvesting, usually in mid-spring for outdoor blanched crops and mid- or late winter for indoor crops. Using a sharp knife, cut the shoots where they join the crown. Discard roots used for forcing indoors; remove all the protective covering from those growing outdoors. The latter can crop for several years, after which they are best replaced from cuttings of the thong-like roots or thin side roots.

Seakale shoots do not keep for any length of time and do not freeze, so use them as soon as possible.

## Varieties
The one mentioned in books is 'Lily White', but it is more a question of finding a supplier than wondering which variety to choose.

# SHALLOTS

Shallots are a close relative of the onion and are treated with reverence in French cuisine. The classic white sauce *beurre blanc* is based on shallot's mild, slightly garlicky flavour. Shallot butter and shallot sauce for steaks are mainstays of French cooking. Elsewhere, small shallots are used for pickling and larger ones as substitutes for onions. As shallots are not readily available in shops and are very easy to grow, they are a better choice than onion for the adventurous gardener with limited space.

### Site and soil

Shallots prefer full sun and well drained, firm, light but moderately fertile soil. If the ground was not enriched for a previous crop, work in well rotted compost in the autumn before planting. If the soil is very acid, lime in midwinter; a week before planting, rake in a general-purpose fertilizer.

### Cultivation

In theory shallots can be grown from seed, but they are almost always grown from sets, mature bulbs which divide to produce eight or more similar sized bulbs by the end of the growing season.

Garden folklore has shallots planted on the shortest day of the year, and harvested on the longest, but late winter or early spring is generally safer for planting. To store shallots awaiting planting, keep them

Shallot
'Dutch Yellow'

# SHALLOTS

in a cool, bright place in a single layer.

Before planting cut off any dried skin from the tops, as birds will use this to pull the sets out of the soil. Plant the sets 20cm (8in) apart in rows 30cm (12in) apart; the tops of the sets should just be visible.

A week or so after planting, check the sets and re-firm any lifted by frost or birds. If necessary, criss-cross black cotton over the rows or use wire-mesh pea guards to deter birds. Keep weeded, but be careful not to damage the sets with a hoe, and water only in dry spells. A mulch of well rotted compost helps keep weeds down and retain soil moisture.

In early summer when the crop begins to ripen, draw back the soil to expose the bulbs fully to the sun.

Shallots suffer from the same afflictions as onions (see page 128) so always buy virus-free sets.

## Harvesting and storing
In midsummer when the leaves turn yellow, lift the crop and separate the bulbs. In dry weather spread them out on the soil surface to dry. In wet weather, spread them out indoors in single layers on wire-mesh racks or newspaper. Finally, remove the stems and any soil still clinging to the bulbs and store in an airy, dry, cool place. Shallots will keep for six months or more; those left at the end of the season can be planted.

## Varieties
'Giant Yellow', 'Long Keeping Yellow' and 'Dutch Yellow' are indistinguishable. 'Dutch Red' and 'Long Keeping Red' are red-skinned equivalents. 'Hâtive de Niort' is a large, brown-skinned variety used for exhibition.

# SORREL

Sorrel, more specifically French sorrel (*Rumex scutatus*), is a tough herbaceous perennial grown for its bitter-tasting leaves. These can be cooked like spinach, or used to make French sorrel soup and sorrel sauce for salmon. Sorrel, like spinach, reduces enormously when cooked, but even a single, finely shredded leaf, adds character to a lettuce salad. Sorrel is related to rhubarb; both contain oxalic acid and should not be eaten in very large quantities.

### Site and soil
French and common sorrel (*R. acetosa*) grow wild, so any well drained soil in sun or light shade will do. However, more tender foliage comes from soil enriched with well rotted compost in the autumn before sowing. Because sorrel is a long-term resident, make sure there are no perennial weeds in the bed.

### Cultivation
Sow in early or mid-spring, either in a seed bed or where it is to grow, in drills 6mm (¼in) deep. Space permanent rows 45cm (18in) apart. When the seedlings are large enough to handle, thin or transplant to 25cm (10in) apart. Water in dry weather and remove any flower spikes that start to form; self-sown seedlings are very prolific and a real nuisance. Every three or four years, lift and divide clumps to keep them vigorous.

### Harvesting and storing
For the first season pick only a few outer leaves from midsummer on. Once plants are established, harvest from early spring to mid-autumn, again picking from the outside and never stripping a plant completely. Young leaves are tender but older leaves are tough. Sorrel wilts soon after picking and should be used as quickly as possible.

Sorrel

161

# SPINACH

Spinach
'Sigmaleaf'

Several types of spinach are grown for their edible leaves. Technically, the 'real' one is winter or prickly-seeded spinach. Summer, or round-seeded spinach, is a close relative with a more delicate flavour. Both are annuals, hardy or nearly so and between them it is possible to harvest spinach all year round. New Zealand spinach, a half-hardy annual, is unrelated to true spinach, though its fleshy mild-flavoured leaves are used as a substitute.

In the garden, spinach is a quick-growing but demanding plant, which expresses displeasure by bolting. In the kitchen, spinach is often overcooked, undercleaned, soggy, bitter and quite unpleasant to eat. To do justice to this much maligned vegetable, serve young leaves fresh in salads, and lightly steam older (but not too old) ones.

### Site and soil
Summer and winter spinach need rich, moisture-retentive but free-draining soil. Dig in well rotted compost in the autumn before planting; if the soil is acid, apply lime in midwinter. A week before sowing, rake in a general-purpose fertilizer.

Winter spinach and first sowings of summer spinach need full sun and shelter. Light shade is better for summer spinach sown from late spring on, since it prevents bolting.

# SPINACH

Grow it in the shade of peas or beans. (Spinach is also a good catch crop.)

New Zealand spinach needs sun and a lime-rich soil; it is tolerant of poor, dry soil and will grow where 'proper' spinach will not.

## Cultivation

Spinach cooks down in bulk, so make generous and successional sowings. For crops from late spring to mid-autumn, start the first crop of summer spinach under cloches in early spring, then sow (without cloches) every two weeks until early summer. Sow winter spinach in late summer and early autumn for harvests from mid-autumn to mid-spring.

Make one sowing of New Zealand spinach, either under glass in mid-spring for planting out after the last frost, or in the open ground in late spring.

Soak all spinach seeds for a few hours before sowing to soften their hard coats. Sow summer and winter spinach, where it is to grow, in drills 2.5cm (1in) deep and 37.5cm (15in) apart. On dry soils make a shallow trench first, 5cm (2in) deep and 25-30cm (10-12in) wide, with the seed drill down the middle. (The trench can be flooded in dry weather). After sowing, cover the seeds with soil, then firm and water if the soil is dry.

New Zealand spinach is large and floppy. Either plant at 75cm (30in) spacings, or sow groups of three seeds at each position and thin to the strongest when the seedlings appear.

Spinach
New Zealand

Crowded seedlings tend to bolt. As soon as possible, thin to 10cm (4in) apart. When the plants touch, thin summer spinach to 30cm (12in) apart and winter spinach to 20cm (8in) apart.

Water generously and regularly; dry conditions and erratic watering cause bolting. Give less water to winter spinach in late summer to discourage lush, vulnerable growth.

Hoe between rows and hand weed between plants. Regularly pinch out the growing tips of New Zealand spinach. Protect winter spinach from mid-autumn on, with cloches or straw. In early spring, apply quick-acting fertilizer.

The most serious problem is spinach blight, caused by the cucumber mosaic virus. Infected leaves turn yellow, shrivel and die, the younger leaves first. Dig up and burn infected plants; eradicate aphids, which transmit the disease.

## Harvesting and storing

Thinnings are the first crop. Pick the outer leaves of mature plants, never more than half the leaves of a plant at any one time. Pinch off young leaves; twist or cut older ones. Winter spinach is slower growing so pick more moderately. Pick the fleshy leaves of New Zealand spinach from the base up.

Spinach can be refrigerated or blanched and frozen, but is best used fresh from the garden.

## Varieties

Summer varieties include the popular 'King of Denmark' and 'Cleanleaf', both of which carry their leaves well above the ground so are less likely to become muddy or gritty. 'Sigmaleaf' is long cropping, bolt-resistant, and can be treated as winter spinach. Winter varieties include 'Monnopa', with a low oxalic acid content, and the extremely hardy 'Broad-Leaved Prickly'. There is only one form of New Zealand spinach.

# SPROUTING SEEDS

Mustard and cress are the most popular, archetypally English, sprouting seeds, but there are others. Because of a more adventurous attitude towards Asian and Oriental cooking, and an increasing awareness of the importance of a healthy diet, sprouting seeds have lost their eccentric connotations. They are rich in vitamins, low in calories, and equally delicious raw or lightly cooked. Cheap to buy and easy to grow, sprouting seeds are foolproof enough for those who lack real gardening instincts.

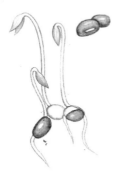

Sprouting seeds
Adzuki

### Site and soil
Use a clean jam jar, but replace its lid with a square of muslin, cheesecloth or old tights held by a rubber band. Alternatively, use a seed tray lined with layered kitchen towels, flannel or a thin layer of peat, as for mustard and cress (see page 125).

### Cultivation
For an ordinary sized jam jar, take a teaspoonful (5ml) of seeds. Wash and rinse them, then soak overnight in lukewarm water. In the morning, drain the seeds and place in the jar. Fill the jar with water, fix the porous fabric in place with the rubber band and drain. Place the jar on its side in a warm, dark place with a minimum temperature of 13°C (53°F). If using a seed tray, dampen the growing medium, then drain the seeds and scatter

Sprouting seeds
Mung

them evenly over it. Keep in a warm, dark spot, as above.

With both methods, the seeds must be kept continually damp or they will dry up and die. Totally sodden conditions, though, lead to rotting. Rinse the seeds in a jar twice a day, morning and evening, draining the water through the lid. Check the dampness of the growing medium in a seed tray daily, and moisten if necessary. The sprouting seeds should remain in the dark if pale, blanched sprouts are preferred. For green sprouts, move the seeds once sprouted to a well lit spot out of direct sunlight.

**Harvesting and storing**
Harvest when the sprouts are the optimum size, which varies according to variety (see below). Use as soon after harvesting as possible.

**Varieties**
Seeds are available from health food stores, seed merchants and supermarkets. Adzuki beans are dark red; the crunchy sprouts are best blanched for three to six days in a dark place and harvested when 2.5cm (1in) long. Sweet-flavoured alfalfa is nicer raw than cooked; use a jar and expose to light once the seeds have sprouted. Harvest when 2.5-5cm (1-2in) long, four or five days after sowing. Fenugreek, a component of curry powder, is grown in the same way as alfalfa. Harvest when 15mm-2.5cm (½-1in) long – the smaller the shoots, the more intense the flavour. Mung beans, or Chinese bean sprouts, are almost as well known as mustard and cress. Sow in a jar and keep dark; the blanched shoots are ready four or five days later when 5cm (2in) long.

Sprouting seeds
Fenugreek

Sprouting seeds
Alfalfa

# SWEDES

Poor swede! Though it is a vegetable grower's dream — hardy, easy going, relatively pest and disease free – it is less popular in the kitchen, and scorned in the dining room. This is because of its association with the very worst, overcooked institutional food, and the fact that in some countries it is grown largely as cattle fodder. In fact, swede has a milder, more subtle taste than turnip to which it is related. (Swede is short for Swedish turnip.) Puréed and mixed with puréed potatoes, swede even could 'pass' as a delectable, *nouvelle cuisine* vegetable.

Swede
'Marian'

### Site and soil
Swede is a member of the brassica family and should never follow another brassica in crop rotation. Like all brassicas, it needs a firm soil, well drained and neutral or slightly alkaline. Choose a sunny spot, if possible. Work well rotted compost into the soil the autumn before sowing and lime if necessary in winter. A week before sowing, rake in a general-purpose fertilizer. In gardens where the soil is heavy and not particularly free draining, or where there is high rainfall, swedes benefit by being grown on 15cm (6in) high, flat-topped ridges.

### Cultivation
Sow the seed thinly in situ in late spring or early summer, in drills 15mm (½in) deep and

45cm (18in) apart. Sowing any earlier than this is pointless, as the plants will either bolt or be ready for harvesting at the height of the summer vegetable season.

Germination usually takes place within two weeks; when the seedlings are large enough to handle, thin them to 25cm (10in) apart. Apart from thinning, there is very little to be done. Water regularly if there is a prolonged drought, otherwise the roots will swell and split when it does rain, and split roots cannot be stored.

Hoe shallowly between the rows to keep weeds down, and hand weed between plants. Be careful of accidentally damaging the roots when hoeing, as such damage allows pests and diseases to enter.

Flea beetle can be troublesome (see Cabbages, page 72) and occasionally swedes are infected with club root (see Brussels Sprouts, page 68). If the soil is poorly drained or over-rich, or if the roots are damaged during hoeing, the fungal infection soft rot will turn them into a slimy pulp. Lift any swedes with suspiciously wilted leaves; destroy if infected.

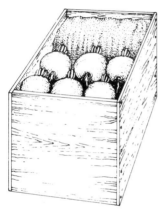

Swedes stored in boxes of peat or sand

**Harvesting**
Young swedes hold no special delights and mature swedes can remain in the ground until needed. For convenience, many people lift the crop towards the end of autumn. Fork carefully under the roots, then twist off the foliage and rub off any soil clinging to the roots. Inspect for damage, then store healthy roots in boxes of

peat or sand kept in a cold, spot. Swedes keep for a week or so refrigerated, but there is little point in using freezer space for them.

Swedes left in the ground over winter will send out pale green shoots the following spring, and these can be used as spring greens. In addition, lifted swedes can be planted in boxes of peat or soil in late autumn or early winter, and induced to produce blanched stems. The process is much the same as for chicory (see page 91); keep the plants in darkness and remember to water them from time to time. Shoots 15-20cm (6-8in) high can be cut.

## Varieties

'Acme' and 'Western Perfection' are both yellow-fleshed, purple-skinned swedes that are quick growing. 'Marian' is also yellow, with a purple skin, and though slower growing, is popular because of its resistance to diseases and root cracking.

# SWEETCORN

In cool, temperate climates, sweetcorn is an unreliable crop, dependent on hot, sunny weather for success. The crop is relatively small for the space it takes so is only worth trying in a large garden.

**Site and soil**
Provide full sun to ripen the crop, and shelter because the plants have shallow root systems and grow to 1.8m (6ft) in height. The ideal soil is rich, sandy, moisture retentive without being waterlogged, and a little on the acid side. If it has not been enriched for a previous crop, dig in well rotted compost the autumn before planting. A week before planting, rake in a general-purpose fertilizer.

**Cultivation**
In favourable gardens, plants can be sown outdoors under cloches in late spring. It is safer, however, to start them under glass in mid-spring. Use peat pots because the roots resent disturbance, and coat the seeds with a dressing first to protect them from soil-borne pests and diseases. Sow two seeds per pot, 2.5cm (1in) deep. Water lightly and provide a temperature of 10°C (50°F) or slightly higher. If both seeds germinate, remove the weaker one. Harden off, then plant out when the threat of frost is over.

Plant sweetcorn in blocks, not rows, to ensure pollination. Space plants 45cm (18in) apart

Sweetcorn

in both directions; the surface of the peat pot should be level with the surface of the surrounding soil. Cloche the plants if the weather turns cold, and protect from birds with black cotton criss-crossed over the soil.

Sweetcorn
'First of All'

Keep well watered and weeded, but be careful of harming the shallow roots when hoeing. Stake the plants if wind is a problem, and gradually earth up soil or mulch round any surface roots that appear. Sometimes side shoots form, but there is no need to remove them.

In midsummer, assist natural wind pollination by gently shaking the male tassels at the top of each plant, so the pollen falls on the female flowers, or 'silks', lower down. When the cobs start to swell, feed with liquid fertilizer.

The maggots of fruit fly cause tattered leaves and stunted, blind growth. Coating the seeds with a seed dressing is the best preventive.

**Harvesting and storing**
Harvest when the tassels are brown and moist; the sheath, still green (not brown or yellow); and the kernels full of creamy fluid. (If the kernels are pierced with a thumbnail, clear fluid indicates an unripe cob; no fluid, an over-ripe one.) Once picked, the sugar content of corn quickly turns to starch, so this crop should really be eaten as soon after picking as possible. Corn can be refrigerated or frozen, but its glorious, just-picked flavour is lost.

**Varieties**
Nearly all are $F_1$ hybrids, which are less risky than old-fashioned varieties. 'First of All' and 'John Innes' are early and reliable; good mid-season varieties include 'Kelvedon' and the similar – some say better – 'Sundance'.

171

# TOMATOES

Tomatoes are one of the first vegetables that anyone with a garden will try to grow; even those without a garden contrive to grow them in window boxes and or on the window sills of modern all-glass office blocks. Although tomatoes in one form or another are part of most daily diets, they weren't always so popular. Until the end of the nineteenth century, tomatoes were grown largely as decorative plants. The fruits were considered harmful, if not downright poisonous, although a few adventurous souls ate tomatoes for dessert.

Botanically, the tomato is a relative of the potato, and, like it, can be killed by a few degrees of frost. On the other hand, it is not a tropical plant and dislikes great heat. It is not a carefree crop, but its needs are predictable, and growing your own tomatoes allows you a wider range of varieties than the perfectly round, red, woolly ones so often sold.

Bush varieties are available that need far less attention than the old-fashioned cordon types, and are a better choice for the casual gardener.

### Site and soil
In the greenhouse or cold frame, tomatoes can be grown directly in the soil, provided it is enriched with well rotted compost in the autumn or winter before planting, and a general-purpose fertilizer raked in a week or so before planting.

Tomatoes

172

Tomato
'Alicante'

Tomato
'Big Boy'

However, tomato pests and diseases are quick to build up in the soil, and unless you are prepared to sterilize it annually, it is better to use grow bags or 25cm (10in) pots filled with a peat-based compost or John Innes potting compost No. 3.

Outdoors, tomatoes need rich, well drained soil, full sun and shelter; the base of a south-facing wall is ideal. In the autumn before planting, incorporate well rotted compost, and a week before, rake in a general-purpose fertilizer. Alternatively use pots or grow bags, as above.

**Cultivation**
If you have a heated greenhouse, sow the appropriate varieties under glass in midwinter. They are normally planted out into pots in late winter and begin cropping in late spring. For an unheated greenhouse, sow in late winter or early spring, plant out in mid- or late spring, and begin harvesting in midsummer. For outdoor varieties, sow under glass in early or mid-spring, plant out in late spring under cloches, or early summer in the open ground, and harvest from late summer onwards.

For large quantities of plants, use seed trays filled with seed compost. Sow thinly and cover lightly with compost, then with black polythene. Maintain a temperature of 16°C (65°F), keep damp and when the seeds germinate, remove the polythene. When the first true leaf appears, prick out into 7.5cm (3in) peat pots. For fewer plants, sow two or three seeds per 7.5cm (3in) peat pot, treat as above, but remove all but the strongest seedling from each pot.

If you buy in young plants instead, choose short-jointed, pot-grown, deep green ones, 15-20cm (6-8in) high.

Transplant seedlings into their permanent positions when the first flower trusses open and the plants are 15-20cm (6-8in) high. Harden off outdoor varieties beforehand, and don't assume that store-bought plants are hardened off.

Copiously water the plant and its permanent position before transplanting. If you have to remove the plant from its pot, support the roots and try to keep the root ball intact. Space open-grown plants 45cm (18in) apart, in rows 90cm (3ft) apart.

Cordon tomatoes need strong supports. Either use bamboo stakes, tying the stem every 20cm (8in); or, for greenhouse cordons, hang fillis from an overhead wire and fix it to a base wire or a wire hook pushed in the soil next to each plant. As the stem grows twist it very carefully around the wire.

Every couple of days, check cordons for sideshoots growing from the leaf axils; pinch them out to prevent wasted energy in the production of unnecessary foliage. Once the fruit are visible on greenhouse cordons, pinch out the growing tips two leaves above the seventh or eighth truss. Pinch out the growing tips of outdoor cordons two leaves above the fourth or fifth truss.

To ensure greenhouse tomato pollination, mist the

Pinching out side shoots of tomatoes

Tomato
'Tigerella'

Tomato
'Golden Sunrise'

plants in the morning, or gently touch the supports to release the clouds of pollen.

Remove the leaves below the lower truss of cordon tomatoes when the fruit has set; remove any yellow leaves as soon as they appear.

Bush tomatoes don't need pinching out, removal of the side shoots or leaves, but they should be mulched with black polythene or straw to keep the fruit off the ground. (In fact, mulching open-grown tomatoes is a good idea anyway to conserve soil moisture and keep down weeds.)

Regular watering is essential but overwatering is fatal. Tomatoes grown in containers and peat-based compost, such as that used in grow bags, need most frequent watering, as much as twice a day.

Containerized plants also need more frequent feeding than open-grown ones. Once the fruit begin to swell use a liquid tomato fertilizer, diluted according to the manufacturer's instructions, every couple of days. Feed open-grown tomatoes weekly.

Give greenhouse tomatoes plenty of ventilation but avoid draughts. Paint the greenhouse with a proprietary sun screen whenever the temperature reaches 27°C (80°F).

The full list of tomato pests, troubles and diseases is too depressing for words. Moth-like whitefly is the most probable pest, with red spider mite a close second under glass. Spray with malathion. Self-descriptive grey mould appears on leaves, stems and fruit. Destroy badly infected plants; improve ventilation and spray the remainder with benomyl. Split fruit is caused by irregular watering. Flowers dropping off and tiny fruits not swelling are caused by pollination failure and excessively dry conditions.

## Harvesting and storing

Tomatoes ripen from the bottom trusses up. Pick when they are firm and just ripe; break the fruit off at the swelling, or 'knuckle', above the calyx. When frost threatens, there are several options. Plants can be dug up and laid on the floor of a greenhouse or on straw under cloches to allow the fruit to ripen.

Alternatively, nearly ripe fruit can be put on a window sill to complete ripening. Green fruit can be wrapped individually in tissue paper, then placed in a drawer or dark cupboard to ripen. (Green tomato chutney is a traditional, and superb, solution to the annual problem of unripe tomatoes.)

Tomato purée can be frozen, or the fresh fruit refrigerated for a few days. Italian sun-dried tomatoes are the latest gourmet craze, but cool temperate climates rarely provide enough sun for such a method of preserving.

## Varieties

Cordon varieties, grown on a single stem, include the following, suitable for greenhouse and garden: the popular and reliable but tasteless 'Moneymaker'; the similar but tastier 'Alicante'; the early and delicious 'Ailsa Craig'; 'MM', a more vigorous and disease-resistant version of 'Moneymaker'; the orange-skinned 'Tangella'; the yellow-skinned 'Golden Sunrise' and earlier 'Yellow Perfection'; and the attractive, red and yellow striped 'Tigerella'.

$F_1$ hybrids for greenhouse growing include the huge, beefsteak 'Big Boy' and slightly smaller 'Supersonic'; the early, disease-resistant 'Shirley'; and 'Eurocross', an early, disease-resistant form.

Cordon varieties for growing outdoors include the old-fashioned, sweet-flavoured, heavy-cropping 'Gardener's Delight' and the early 'Outdoor Girl'.

Outdoor bush varieties, requiring no stopping or staking, include the window-box size 'Tiny Tim'; the early, dependable 'Sigmabush'; the heavy-cropping 'Sleaford Abundance' and the new, highly recommended 'Red Alert'. For fun, grow mixed ornamental tomatoes in a variety of colours and diminutive shapes.

# TURNIPS

Turnip, an easy-going
of the brassica family, is
vegetable of many parts.
quick-maturing roots are a s
and summer treat, small and
delicately flavoured. Maincrop
turnips have larger, coarser
roots, both in texture and
flavour, that are ready in mid-
autumn for late autumn and
winter use. Lastly, late summer
sowings of maincrop turnips
provide turnip tops, or spring
greens, the following spring.

People often shun turnips,
regarding them as little more
than cattle fodder, but the
French have a much higher
regard for this crop and
considerable space is devoted
to it in French cookery books.
The slightly sweet, slightly
peppery flavour and crisp
texture of turnip are used to
complement rich meat and
poultry. Young roots are served
whole, either glazed or
garnished with parsley. Older
ones are thickly peeled,
quartered and boiled, then
puréed with potato, or added
to stews, casseroles or soups.

In a small garden, growing
maincrop turnips makes little
sense for they are readily
available and inexpensive.
Though more difficult to grow,
early turnips are better to eat
and really benefit from being
freshly picked.

Turnip
'Jersey Navet'

## Site and soil
Turnips should never follow
another brassica crop. The
ideal soil is neutral or alkaline,
fertile but not recently

Turnip
'Snowball'

Turnip
'Purple-Topped Milan'

enriched, and moisture-retentive but free draining. Ground used previously for potatoes is particularly suitable. If the ground has not been enriched for the previous crop, work in well rotted compost the autumn before sowing. (Fresh compost or manure leads to mis-shapen roots.) Lime, if necessary, in winter. A week before sowing, rake in a general-purpose fertilizer.

Early crops need full sun and shelter. In summer it is easier to grow turnips where the temperatures are cool and the rainfall high, though some varieties are especially bolt-resistant.

**Cultivation**
Make the earliest sowings in late winter, under cloches or cold frames, for a late spring crop. As with all quick-maturing crops, sow little and often to avoid a glut. Sow second-early turnips outdoors in early spring. If your garden is large, continue sowing at two-weekly intervals until late summer, for crops from late spring to mid-autumn. If your garden is small, omit summer sowings and use the space for more typically summer crops such as tomatoes, peas and beans.

Sow maincrop turnips in mid- and late summer for harvesting from mid-autumn onwards. Sow turnips grown for greens in late summer and early autumn for harvesting the following spring.

Turnips, like other root vegetables, don't transplant well. Sow them where they are to mature, in drills 15mm (½in) deep and 30cm (12in) apart for maincrops, 25cm (10in) apart for early turnips and spring greens. Water the seed bed thoroughly first if the soil is dry. Broadcast sowing — simply scattering the seeds — is sometimes advocated for spring greens, but weeding then becomes a problem as hoes can't be used.

Sow thinly, cover with soil and firm. Germination usually takes a week or ten days. As soon as possible, begin thinning in stages, first to 5cm (2in) apart. Thin spring greens again, to 10cm (4in) apart; early turnips should eventually be 15cm (6in) apart and maincrops 25-30cm (10-12in) apart. Use the larger thinnings in the kitchen as spring greens.

Early open-grown crops should be cloched or protected with straw if the weather turns cold. Hoe and hand weed as necessary to keep weeds down and the soil from becoming compacted. Be careful not to damage the roots while hoeing. A steady supply of water is essential to prevent the plants running to seed before forming roots, or forming split, cracked roots.

Flea beetle is a particular problem; dust with derris if small, round holes appear on the leaves; seedlings are most vulnerable. Scatter slug pellets if slugs are troublesome. They eat the roots as well as the leaves, leaving the plants vulnerable to secondary infections such as soft rot and dry rot. In both cases, infected plants should be lifted and destroyed as there is no cure.

Turnip
'Green-Top White'

**...ng and storing**
...y turnips as needed,
... them out by their
...e. The roots should be
...cm (2-3in) in diameter.
...ery small ones can be served
...aw, either grated or sliced in
salads.) Early turnips keep for a
week or slightly more
refrigerated and can be frozen,
but are best used immediately.

Lift maincrop turnips as
needed from mid-autumn
onwards, using a garden fork.
Some varieties are hardier than
others; in mild areas, where

the ground is not needed for
spring sowing or planting,
leave hardy turnips in situ.
Otherwise, lift the whole crop
in mid- or late autumn. Twist
off the foliage, leaving a little
stump, wipe off the soil and
store the roots in boxes of peat
or sand, kept in a cool place.
They will keep right through
the winter.

Harvest turnip tops in early
or mid-spring. The smooth,
blue-grey leaves are at their
best when 10-15cm (4-6in)
high. A second crop of leaves
should follow the first; once
the flower stalks appear, lift
and compost the roots. If pests
have been troublesome, burn
the roots instead.

**Varieties**
Early round varieties include
the quick-growing, popular
'Snowball' and the similar
'Early Six Weeks'; the larger,
red-topped 'Red Globe' and
the white, $F_1$ hybrid 'Tokyo
Cross', normally sown later
than other earlies.

Flat-topped varieties include
the early 'Purple-Topped
Milan' and its even earlier
strain 'Sprinter'. An unusual
but delicious flat-top turnip is
the yellow-fleshed 'Golden
Perfection'. 'Jersey Navet'
('navet' being French for
turnip) is the most usual
cylindrical variety, good for
very early sowings.

Maincrop turnips are large
and round, and include several
green-tops: 'Green-Top
White', grown for its leaves,
'Arca' and the very hardy
'Manchester Market'. 'Golden
Ball' is a compact, yellow-
fleshed form.

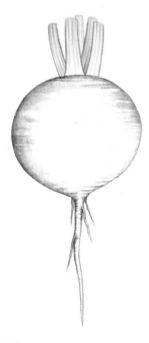

Turnip
'Golden Ball'

# WATERCRESS

Watercress, the standard garnish, salad vegetable and main ingredient of that most delectable of starters, cream of watercress soup, is worth growing only out of curiosity.

## Site and soil
Watercress grows wild in shallow, fast-flowing water. Even if you are lucky enough to have such a feature in your garden, there is a risk of liver fluke infesting the crop, especially if cattle or sheep use the water upstream. (Never pick watercress from the wild for this reason.)

Instead, choose an open, lightly shaded spot near a source of water. Dig a trench 60-90cm (2-3ft) square and 30cm (12in) deep. Place a 15cm (6in) thick layer of well rotted compost in the bottom, topped with a 7.5cm (3in) layer of soil.

## Cultivation
Theoretically, seed can be sown in the trench in mid-spring. Realistically, seed is harder to come by than cuttings from a greengrocer. Some shoots will already have roots, others can be encouraged by placing the shoots in a glass of water. When roots have formed, flood the trench and when the water has seeped away, plant the shoots, 5cm (2in) apart in each direction.

Daily watering is vital, and so is removing any weed seedlings that appear in these lush conditions.

## Harvesting and storing
Cut, don't pull, the tops of the plants; this encourages more side shoots to form. Though perennial, constant cropping wears out the plants, but they can easily be replaced with fresh stock. Watercress wilts soon after picking and is best used immediately.

Watercress

# HERBS

Herbs are jacks-of-all trade, and have a long, intriguing and speckled history. Over the centuries, herbs have been gathered from the wild and cultivated for medicinal, magical and religious purposes, as well as for culinary ones. Herbs are steeped in the folklore of widely different cultures, and there is often an element of scientific truth in herbal folk remedies.

Herbs feature in books on ornamental gardening as often as they do in books on vegetable gardening. They are not, however, showy or colourful plants. Some are actually ugly; tarragon, for example, looks very much like a weed but its fresh flavour is exquisite, a culinary pearl beyond price.

Those fortunate enough to have a kitchen garden can grow rows of herbs without any reference to garden design; or they can attempt a traditional *potager*, a kitchen garden in which the various crops are laid out in an attractive geometric pattern.

Herb gardens proper – patches of land devoted solely or largely to herbs – are usually ornamental. In Tudor and Elizabethan knot gardens, dwarf hedging of box, lavender or cotton lavender was laid out in geometric patterns based on intersecting circles and squares. The herbs were then grown in the compartments. As well as providing a winter skeleton (herb gardens in winter look very barren), such hedging keeps highly invasive herbs away from more delicate ones.

A modern solution is the chequerboard herb garden. The 'red squares' are precast concrete slabs, the 'black squares' open ground, with a different herb growing in each one. On a smaller, more dainty scale there is the wagon-wheel herb garden. Half-sink an old cart wheel in the ground, then plant a different herb in each of the sections between the spokes. Sink gardens, trough gardens, tubs, flower pots and window boxes are all possible homes for herbs, but the smaller they are, the more careful the choice and combination of herbs must be, and the more frequent the watering.

Finally, herbs are delightful in mixed borders, where their subdued tones are often a welcome relief and a good setting for more intensely coloured ornamental plants.

Much is made of growing herbs as close as possible to the house for the sake of convenience. This may suit the cook, but not the herbs. While a few tolerate or even prefer shade and damp soil, most herbs are Mediterranean in origin and need full sun to thrive and develop their essential oils. They also need light, free-draining soil, and shelter. Siting herbs should be a sensible compromise between the cook and the plants. But given suitable conditions, herbs are among the easiest plants to grow.

Growing herbs on a sunny kitchen window sill is possible, but the low light levels in winter, combined with hot, steamy atmosphere at a time when the plants are normally resting, make it a difficult long-term proposition. Digging up annuals and tender perennial herbs before the first frost and taking them indoors will give a pleasantly extended, but not indefinite, supply of fresh leaves.

Most people enjoy the idea of being self sufficient to some extent. Even those who lack the room or inclination to grow vegetables get great pleasure from picking a few sprigs of home-grown mint to cook with new potatoes, or a sprig of parsley for garnish. Growing herbs is often the only feasible form of self sufficiency for city dwellers – a vital, if slender, link with the natural world.

## Preserving herbs

Herbs enliven many dishes and even the most ordinary meal may be enormously improved by the imaginative, even lavish, use of herbs. Yet their value does not lie in their taste alone. Nowadays, the presentation of food is almost as important as the taste, and fresh herbs, finely chopped or placed on the side of the plate in large sprigs, please the eye as well as the palate.

For decoration, fresh herbs are more valuable than dried ones. Evergreen herbs can be used fresh all year round, while annuals and deciduous perennial herbs can be potted up at the end of the growing season and brought indoors to extend the supply into winter. Herbs unsuitable for potting are those with long tap-roots and, obviously, those with very large habits of growth.

In the depths of winter, preserved herbs become a seasonal necessity; and the process of harvesting and preserving home-grown herbs is one of the pleasures of summer. Timing varies from herb to herb, but the leaves are at their best, with the highest concentration of essential oils, before the flower buds open. Using scissors or secateurs, harvest the sprigs on a dry, sunny day in the morning, when the dew is gone, but before the sun is at its hottest. Don't collect the herbs in a plastic bag and then leave them inside it to steam for hours. Don't pick wild herbs; some poisonous plants resemble garden herbs, and other wild plants are protected by law. Don't denude a herb of foliage if you want a continuing supply of fresh leaves from that plant. Take up to half the foliage; midsummer pruning often stimulates herbs to produce a second spurt of growth.

Drying is the traditional method of preservation, but herbs such as chervil, parsley and chives, with thin leaves or elusive flavours, are better frozen than dried. Those with thick leaves and strong flavours, such as sage and summer savory, do dry well and their flavour and aroma are intensified in the process. In cooking, use half the amount of dried herbs as you would fresh.

Tie the sprigs in loose bunches, then hang upside down in a well ventilated, dark, dry, warm spot. The leaves will wilt and shrivel; when they are totally crisp and dry, they can be stripped from the stalks, crumbled and stored. Drying time varies, but can take three weeks or more.

Alternatively, spread the sprigs out to dry in a single layer on a wire mesh rack, placed in an airing cupboard or above a night storage heater. Turn the herbs over regularly to ensure even drying.

Herbs can be dried in a very low oven with the door left ajar, but the herbs are liable to cook instead of dry and the flavour and aroma suffer.

Store each herb separately, in an airtight jar. Purists insist on darkness, as light slowly fades colour and weakens flavour, but, on a practical level, the herbs should be within easy reach for cooking, and rows of herb jars look pretty on display. Even less purist, and prettier still, is to hang dried bunches from shelves or overhead beams. Keep the bunches well away from the cooker as steam rots the leaves.

Frozen herbs retain their colour and flavour, but lose their texture so are useless as decorative garnish. Use the same quantity of frozen as fresh herbs when cooking.

The ice-cube method of freezing is popular. Blanch then chop the leaves and loosely pack them into ice trays. Fill with water, freeze solid and transfer into polythene bags. Defrosting the cubes is unnecessary; simply add from the dish while cooking. It is quicker and less messy, though, to simply wash and pat dry the herbs, chop roughly and place into polythene bags, then seal and freeze them. With this method the herbs tend to be less mushy and wilted when defrosted.

Make sure frozen herbs are stored in airtight containers, or their aroma may taint other frozen goods.

To dry seeds, pick the whole head just as it starts to change from yellow to brown. Ripe seeds will be scattered by the least touch, and the object of the exercise defeated. Put several heads upside down in a paper bag, then hang the bag in a warm, dry, airy spot. Once the seeds have ripened and fallen to the bottom of the bag, collect and store in airtight containers. Harvesting can take several weeks, as the seeds don't always ripen at the same time.

# ANGELICA

A cottage-garden herb of long standing, *Angelica archangelica* can reach a height of 1.8m (6ft) or more and as much across. It is a stately plant, with large, deeply indented, light-green leaves and flat heads of greenish white flowers, like those of cow parsley to which angelica is related. It is attractive enough to be grown in the back of a mixed border, if there is sufficient space.

Angelica usually behaves like a biennial, flowering in the second, or sometimes third, year after germination then dying. If the flower bud is removed, the plant's life is extended. Unlike most herbs, angelica prefers rich, moist soil and some shade, though it tolerates other growing conditions.

Seed will not germinate unless it is very fresh; it is safest to buy a young plant or sow seed freshly gathered from a neighbour or friend's angelica. Never collect seed from the wild. Angelica resembles hemlock (*Conium maculatum*) which is deadly poisonous. Sow seed in drills 2.5cm (1in) deep in mid- or late spring then transplant to its final position in autumn. An established angelica will seed itself freely, and unwanted seedlings must be ruthlessly removed if they are not to take over the garden.

Young stems and stalks are used to make candied angelica. The leaves, which dry easily, make an aromatic tisane, and oil distilled from the roots and seeds is used to flavour Chartreuse, anisette and other liqueurs.

Angelica
*Angelica archangelica*

# BALM

Balm (*Melissa officinalis*), or lemon balm, is not a particularly beautiful herb and yet no cottage garden was without it. Then, as now, its popularity was derived from its sweet, lemony scent and its attractiveness to bees.

(Beekeepers traditionally rub their hives with balm to keep bees from straying.)

Balm is a tough, herbaceous perennial, needing only protection from the hardest frosts and watering in prolonged dry spells. It is a good herb for containerized growing and can be propagated by dividing the roots of an established plant in autumn or spring, or from seed. Happy in sun or light shade, balm quickly increases by means of its invasive roots and can eventually become a nuisance. It seeds itself freely and seedlings are often found some distance from the parent plant. The upright stems, which carry tiny white flowers in summer, reach a height of 60cm (2ft). After flowering the leaves become coarse and tatty looking, and some people remove the flower stalks as soon as they start to develop. In any case, they are cut back in autumn to tidy the garden for winter.

There is a smaller, more well behaved form, *M.o.* 'Aurea', with attractive, yellow-variegated leaves. Its seedlings, however, often revert to green, and it is slightly less robust than the species.

Freshly picked balm leaves are used to flavour salads, summer drinks and poultry dishes. Dried leaves can be made into a tea, or a few added to a pot of ordinary tea. They are also standard ingredients in pot-pourri and herbal pillows.

Balm
*Melissa officinalis*

# BASIL

Although all herbs are better when used fresh, there is a special intensity about the flavour of fresh basil. Since it is not easily available in shops, serious cooks usually grow their own.

Basil
*Ocimium basilicum*

The most popular form of this half-hardy annual is sweet basil (*Ocimium basilicum*), which makes a loose-growing, multi-stemmed plant up to 60cm (2ft) high. Its large, soft leaves are a fresh green, though there is a form, *O.b.* 'Dark Opal', with purple leaves. Slightly hardier and more suitable for container growing, is bush basil, *O. minimum*. It makes a much smaller plant, with smaller, denser leaves.

Sow the seed indoors in early or mid-spring. A sunny window sill or heated propagator kept at 15°C (60°F) will ensure germination within two weeks. Harden off the young plants before planting out after the last frost. Choose a sunny, sheltered spot with free-draining, reasonably rich soil, and keep the plants well watered. If more than one is being grown, space the plants 25-30cm (10-12in) apart.

All basils have a tendency to get leggy, but frequent pinching out of the tips and removing all flower buds will encourage bushy growth. (Use the tips in the kitchen; don't throw them away.) If the weather turns cold and frost threatens, protect the plants with cloches or large, upturned empty jars. If you want to prolong the season, carefully lift and pot up healthy plants before the first autumn frost. Cut back the growth by half and place the pot on a sunny window sill.

# BAY

Unlike other herbs, bay (*Laurus nobilis*) may reach great heights: 18m (60ft) or more in its native Mediterranean environment. In Northern Europe, however, it is usually seen as a small, pyramidal bush a tenth of that height. Bay is slow growing and ideal for containers. It also stands

Bay
*Laurus nobilis*

training well, and is often seen clipped into a standard 'lollipop' tree or formal cone. (Such plants are extremely expensive.)

Bay can be propagated by layering or taking cuttings, but these are both very slow processes and two years may pass before roots form. For all practical purposes, buy the largest plant you can afford from a garden centre. Plant in a sunny, sheltered spot; well drained soil is essential.

Water in dry weather for the first year or two until the plant has become established, and protect from hard frost by surrounding it with straw or sacking. Cold winds and prolonged frost can turn the shiny, dark leaves a dismal brown, or kill the above-ground growth altogether. While the bay usually recovers and sends out new leaves or new shoots from the base, it may take many years to reach its previous size. In the case of formally trained trees this is a disaster. Bays grown in containers are particularly vulnerable and should be moved into a cool frost-free place, such as a greenhouse or conservatory, for the winter months. Containerized bays also need frequent watering in the growing season.

Bay is an essential ingredient of *bouquet garni*, used to flavour stews, sauces, soups and marinades. It is also used to flavour sweet dishes such as milk puddings and custards.

# BERGAMOT

Bergamot
*Monarda didyma*

Equally at home in a herbaceous border or herb garden, bergamot (*Monarda didyma*) is also known as bee balm because of its attractiveness to bees. It is sometimes called Oswego tea after the American Oswego Indians who used its leaves to make a refreshing drink.

Bergamot is a perennial, usually grown in the form 'Cambridge Scarlet', which has rich red, hooded flowers. There are other named forms with pink, salmon, white or pale blue flowers, all of which appear in summer. (Removing the faded flowers helps prolong the display.) It is related to the mint family and its leaves are pointed and mint-like.

Bergamot is an easy plant to care for, provided it is never allowed to dry out. Mulch in spring with well rotted compost, and cut down the 1m (3ft) high stems after flowering in autumn. Propagation is by division of the roots in spring.

Both the fresh young leaves and the flowers make an excellent, last-minute addition to salads. The pungent flavour of the leaves helps counteract the richness of pork as well, so they can be used instead of sage or rosemary. When dried, the leaves and flowers are used in pot-pourri and sachets. Oil of bergamot, which is used in perfume, comes, confusingly, from the bergamot orange, *Citrus bergamia*.

# BORAGE

Borage (*Borago officinalis*) is well known for its delightful, intensely blue flowers, which appear in drooping clusters through the summer months and, occasionally, at other times of the year. Pink- and white-flowered forms are rare natural occurrences.

The plant itself, a hardy annual, is quite ordinary looking, with hollow, hairy stems and rough, equally hairy leaves. Heights range from 30 to 75cm (12 to 30in). In the days when people had wild gardens, borage was often grown there so that space in the garden proper could be given to more refined-looking herbs. Nevertheless, borage earns its keep. It is very attractive to bees which, lured by borage, can pollinate garden crops nearby. Its young leaves have a strong cucumber flavour and, cut before they become coarse and hairy, are delicious in salads, soups, claret cups and other fruit drinks. The flowers are also put in drinks, can be crystallized, or dried for pot-pourris. (The leaves do not dry well.)

Borage prefers a sunny, dry spot and slightly impoverished soil. Sow in spring, covering the seed with 15mm (½in) of soil. Keep the seedlings free of weeds and thin them to 30cm (12in) apart.

After that, the only requirement is to root out unwanted seedlings; there is an old saying that once you have borage, you always have borage. One good point is that self-sown seedlings, germinating in autumn, provide young leaves through the winter months.

Borage
*Borago officinalis*

# CARAWAY

The seeds of caraway (*Carum carvi*) are the traditional flavouring for rye breads, cooked apple dishes, sauerkraut and cheeses. Less well known is the fact that young caraway leaves can be used in much the same way as

Caraway
*Carum carvi*

fresh parsley to garnish and flavour salads, stews and cooked vegetables. In former times, the long white taproots of caraway were boiled and eaten like carrots; then, as now, oil of caraway seed was used to flavour kümmel, the German liqueur named after caraway.

A biennial of the *Umbelliferae* family, caraway is best sown in late summer, in a dry, well-drained, lightly shaded spot. (Seed can be sown in spring to flower two summers later, but it is generally thought to be riskier.) Sow in situ, then thin the seedlings to a spacing of 25-30cm (10-12in) apart. There is little cultivation needed as caraway is perfectly hardy and tolerant of dry conditions.

The following summer the plant will produce a 60cm (2ft) high flower stalk, topped by typical, lacy, white umbelliferous flowers. These should be gathered when the seed is ripe, from midsummer onwards, and put upside down in paper bags to dry. Alternatively, lay the heads in a single layer on a tray placed over a very low source of heat, such as a night storage heater or recently turned-off cooker. When the flowers have shed their seeds, these should be stored in airtight glass jars. Some of the seed can be sown the following summer, although it is likely that self-sown seedlings will appear in the garden of their own accord.

# CHERVIL

A modest-looking herb, chervil (*Anthriscus cerefolium*) is much loved by the French who use it in *fines herbes* mixtures. It is a delicate, fern-like plant (though actually a member of the *Umbelliferae* family) and cannot be dried successfully. For the full flavour – peppery, with a hint of aniseed – chervil must be used fresh and added at the very last moment as it quickly wilts once picked.

Chervil
*Anthriscus cerefolium*

There is a plain-leaved chervil, but the curly-leaved form is more popular and is the one usually offered in seed catalogues. It can be grown as an annual or biennial, and reaches a height of up to 60cm (2ft). Chervil is a relatively quick-growing herb, taking just two months from sowing for the first leaves to be ready for picking. Sow seeds outdoors from spring through the end of summer; late sowings will provide fresh chervil during the winter months. Well drained soil and a lightly shaded spot are best during warmer weather, but full sun is appreciated by plants growing in winter. The traditional way round this dilemma is to sow chervil between rows of summer vegetables. The latter provide shade when it is necessary, but are cleared once the cold weather sets in.

Keep chervil well watered. Heat and dry soil cause it to bolt – send up a flower stalk prematurely – after which its flavour diminishes. Remove the flower stalk as soon as it starts to grow, unless you want seedlings for next year's crop.

Chervil can be grown in a container as long as it is watered regularly. Whether open-grown or pot-grown, it should be harvested by cutting the outer leaves, leaving the central growing point intact.

Chervil soup is a classic dish, but the herb is also excellent for egg, poultry and salad dishes.

# CHIVES

Often grown as an edging plant, chives (*Allium schoenoprasum*) are among the prettiest and most useful of herbs. Their mild, oniony flavour, neat, grassy leaves, and mauve pincushion flowers make them prime candidates for the herb garden, flower pot or window box. To get the best flavour and texture, the flower buds should be nipped off (this applies to most herbs). The flowers themselves can be used as garnish, though not eaten; faded flowers should always be removed.

Chives are perennial plants, evergreen in mild climates, deciduous in harsh ones. Though they can be grown from seed, it is easier to buy young plants. Plant them in spring, about 25cm (10in) apart, in a moisture-retentive, rich soil in sun or light shade. Keep the ground free of weeds until the clumps knit together, and water well in dry weather. The plants quickly form huge clumps, which need lifting and dividing every few years.

Chives are traditional companion plants. Some gardeners site them near rows of carrots so their oniony aroma can mask the smell of the carrots and so discourage carrot fly.

Pick the leaves regularly to encourage new growth, cutting them just above ground level. The snipped leaves can be used to flavour salads, egg dishes and cream cheese — any dish, in fact, which would be improved by a hint of onion. Chives do not dry well. In autumn, lift and pot up a clump to grow on a window sill during the winter.

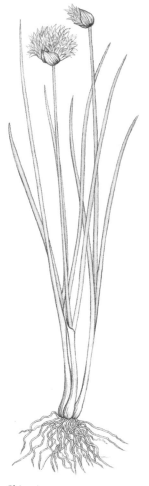

Chives
*Allium schoenoprasum*

# CORIANDER

Another member of the *Umbelliferae* family, coriander (*Coriandrum sativum*) is a staple ingredient of Chinese, Indian and Middle Eastern cooking. Its coarse, parsley-like leaves are used to impart a strong, pungent flavour to salads, casseroles and soups. Its ripe, pale, round seeds are one of the components of curry, and in Thai cuisine the roots are ground with garlic and used to flavour meat. Coriander seeds are also familiar to Western cooks, essential to English pickling spices and used for flavouring chutneys, apple pies and, curiously enough, gin. A very versatile plant, coriander is worth growing because fresh leaves are not easily available from shops, and dried coriander leaves are not worth using.

Coriander is a hardy annual with pink-tinged, round, lacy flowers in summer. Sow the seed thinly in a sunny spot from mid-spring onwards. Light, well drained soil is ideal. If the plants are grown for their leaves alone, thin the seedlings to about 7.5cm (3in) apart. If the seed is to be harvested, leave 20cm (8in) between plants. (Unripe seed is not pleasant to eat, however, and in cool, wet summers it may not ripen.)

Take only a few outer leaves at a time, snipping them off close to ground level. To gather ripe seed, collect the seed heads at the end of summer and put them upside down in a paper bag. Leave the bag in a dry, warm spot for two weeks, by which time the seeds will have collected in the bottom. Transfer to a dry, airtight jar. Coriander seeds retain their flavour and fertility for a long time and, properly stored, can be successfully germinated the following year.

Theoretically, coriander can be grown in large containers, but its 60cm (2ft) high leaves are not particularly pretty, and there are other, more suitable candidates.

Coriander
*Coriandrum sativum*

# DILL

Perhaps best known as a constituent of dill pickles, dill (*Peucedanum graveolens*) is an easy annual to grow, requiring little more than full sun and well drained soil. Its feathery, 1m (3ft) high foliage is a fresh green and its flat heads of yellow-green flowers are as valuable in the ornamental garden as they are in the kitchen. They are equally good for cutting, their cool colour contrasting well with the hot pink and red roses of summer.

Sow seed, where it is to grow, from mid-spring onwards in drills 6mm (¼in) deep. Keep the seedlings watered in dry weather and thin them to 30cm (12in) apart. The thinnings can be used in the kitchen. Mature plants rarely need watering as they send down long taproots.

Foliage should be ready for picking about two months after sowing. Use its anise-like flavour to enhance poultry, egg, salad and rice dishes. Fish, particularly, marries well with dill, and dill and salmon is a classic combination.

Though the foliage is prettier, it is the seeds that have the more intense flavour, and they retain more of their flavour when dried. Towards the end of summer, when the flower heads turn brown, place them upside down in a paper bag and leave for about two weeks in a warm, dry place. When the seeds are dry, store them in an airtight glass jar. Sprinkle them on breads and rolls, or use as a substitute for caraway seed. Dill water is used to remedy wind in babies, though it is easier bought than made.

Any seed heads left on the plant will ensure a crop of dill seedlings the following summer.

Dill
*Peucedanum graveolens*

# FENNEL

Dill and fennel are often confused as they both look and taste similar. In fact, fennel (*Foeniculum vulgare*) is a perennial, while dill is an annual. Fennel is stronger growing, reaching a height of 1.8m (6ft) compared to dill's 1m (3ft), and it is more strongly flavoured. (Florence fennel or finocchio, *F. v. dulce*, is a bulbous vegetable, discussed on pages 101-102.)

Fennel is a tough plant, and can be found growing wild in coastal areas and stony wasteland. In the garden, free draining soil and a sunny, sheltered spot are ideal; in exposed gardens, fennel may need staking. Sow the seed where it is to grow from early spring onwards; thin the seedlings to 30cm (12in) apart. Young plants can be bought from garden centres and, of course, established clumps can be propagated by lifting and dividing in spring.

The hair-like leaves do not dry well, though they can be blanched and then frozen in ice cubes. Use the fresh leaves to flavour egg dishes, cheese dishes, salads and fish – fennel with mackerel or mullet is traditional. The young shoots can be boiled and eaten like a vegetable, and older, tougher stalks can be used as a bed on which to grill fish.

Collect fennel seeds in early autumn, just before they turn brown. Dry and store as for dill (see opposite). Any ripe seed heads left on the plant inevitably means nearby seedlings the following year.

Fennel, particularly the beautiful bronze-leaved form *F. v. purpurea*, is pretty enough to be grown at the back of a mixed border.

Fennel
*Foeniculum vulgare*

# GARLIC

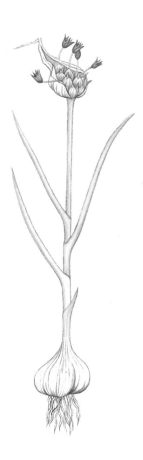

Garlic (*Allium sativum*) is too well known to need description. Its fat white cloves are used to flavour salad dressings and meat and vegetable dishes; garlic bread is a staple offering in many restaurants. Garlic's anti-social reputation comes from the unpleasant smell that fresh garlic leaves on the breath. The longer garlic is cooked, however, the mellower and less offensive its effect on the breath so quite large quantities can be used safely.

An ordinary head of garlic, with plump, unshrivelled cloves, can be taken apart and planted from late winter through mid-spring. Choose a sunny spot with rich, well drained soil. Plant the cloves, right-way up and with their silvery skins still intact, at 15cm (6in) intervals and 5cm (2in) deep. Keep the weeds down and water only in the case of prolonged drought.

Towards the end of summer, when the 45cm (18in) high leaves start to turn yellow, harvest the garlic. Use a fork to lift the bulbs, then leave them on the surface of the soil for a few days to dry. If the weather is wet, take the bulbs indoors and dry them in a single layer on a window sill. When dry, hang the garlic in bunches or pretty garlic ropes in the kitchen. The best cloves can be saved for planting the following spring for although garlic is a perennial, it is always treated as an annual.

Garlic
*Allium sativum*

# HORSERADISH

Horseradish is not a herb for those with small gardens. It is an almost indestructible perennial plant (*Armoracia rusticana*) with very tenacious habits; in Britain, it is a naturalized weed of waste places and roadsides. Also, by no stretch of the imagination is horseradish pretty, even in summer when its tiny white flowers are carried on 1.2m (4ft) high stems. Its dock-like, inedible leaves are dull-looking and often become brown-edged as summer progresses.

Why grow it? Freshly grated horseradish root is irreplacable as an accompaniment to roast beef, and horseradish cream is a delicious complement to fish dishes. Horseradish can be used to flavour vinegars and pickles and, more pragmatically, it will grow where little else will.

In spring, plant the thin side roots, about 6mm (¼in) in diameter, in holes spaced 45cm (18in) apart. Place each root vertically in the hole, then cover with 15cm (6in) of topsoil and keep weeded until the horseradish's leaves grow big enough to smother all competition.

In autumn, dig up the roots and store in sand-filled boxes until needed. The root system is strong and extensive, extending 60cm (2ft) or more into the soil. Many gardening books advocate clearing the site completely, but tiny bits of root are inevitably left and these will send up new leaves the following spring. Roots for initial planting can be had from garden centres, or from a friend's garden. Once horseradish is established in a garden, the thin side roots can be stored over winter, then planted. Deliberately leaving horseradish in the ground is not a good idea as the quality of the roots deteriorates and the plant will take over more and more of the garden.

Horseradish
*Armoracia rusticana*

199

# HYSSOP

Some books list hyssop (*Hyssopus officinalis*) as a perennial plant, others list it as a shrub or sub-shrub. It is multi-stemmed and quite woody near the base, but is rather short-lived and a harsh winter can be fatal. Whatever its botanical definition, hyssop is a neat, well behaved and attractive plant. To bees and butterflies it is irresistible, and it deserves a place in a herb garden for this reason alone.

Hyssop was used as a culinary herb far more in medieval times than it is today. With its slightly bitter flavour, a mixture of mint, rosemary and savory, it is an adventurous choice to enhance stews, salads, fruit pies and stuffings.

The tiny, two-lipped tubular flowers which make a pretty garnish are carried in whorls on the terminal spikes and bloom over many weeks in summer. Colours vary from rose pink through a mauvy purple, but *H.o.* 'Albus' has white flowers and *H.o.* 'Roseus' has pale pink ones.

Hyssop needs full sun, a light, well drained soil, and shelter. It can be grown from seed sown in mid-spring, or from cuttings taken in late spring, but it is much easier to buy young plants, which are relatively inexpensive. Hyssop was a traditional edging plant for herb gardens and knot gardens; if used for edging it should be spaced 25cm (10in) apart. Its dense, rather upright growth reaches a height of 60cm (2ft). Prune back by half in mid-spring to encourage bushy growth, and deadhead to encourage the production of flowers.

Hyssop
*Hyssopus officinalis*

# LEMON VERBENA

This semi-hardy, deciduous shrub is a relatively recent addition to the herb garden, having been discovered in Chile in the late eighteenth century. Lemon verbena (*Lippia citriodora*) is a curiously passive herb; its intensely fragrant lemon scent is only released if the leaves are touched or bruised. For this reason it is often grown by a path or next to a terrace or door, instantly accessible to those passing by. It is also often seen against south-facing walls, whose shelter and latent heat are necessary for the plant's survival. Against a wall, lemon verbena can reach a height of 3m (10ft); grown in a container, it is considerably smaller.

Lemon verbena is normally propagated from cuttings taken in summer and rooted in a heated propagator, but buying a small plant in late spring after the last frosts is more sensible. It needs sun, shelter and free-draining soil. Keep it well watered in dry weather, remembering that the soil next to a wall is drier than that in the rest of the garden. In autumn, protect the roots and base of the plant from frost with a layer of compost, straw or sacking. In cold, exposed gardens, grow lemon verbena in a pot small enough to be taken indoors for the winter months. A gently heated sunroom, greenhouse or conservatory is ideal. (Do not be tempted to keep it in a warm room, hoping that it will remain evergreen. Its health will deteriorate rapidly.)

In mid-spring, prune the side shoots to within 2.5cm (1in) of the main branches and remove the protective covering. The lance-shaped leaves that follow can be used to flavour summer salads and drinks; dried, the leaves add a lemony scent to a pot of tea or pot-pourri mixture.

Lemon verbena
*Lippia citriodora*

# LOVAGE

Lovage (*Levisticum officinale*) is a coarse-looking herb, related to dill and fennel but without their delicate appearance. It is also a large-scale plant, its red stems reaching a height of 1.8m (6ft) or more. Realistically, there is no place for lovage in a small or dainty herb garden, in a containerized herb garden, or in an ornamental border.

In defence of lovage, it is an undemanding perennial, tolerant of light shade and tough enough to smother any weeds that encroach upon its territory. For those with huge herb gardens and the collecting instinct of a botanist, or for those with semi-wild patches in their garden, lovage is worth considering. Its strong, celery-like flavour is useful for soups, stews and casseroles; lovage soup is a traditional recipe. The young leaves can be finely chopped and added to summer salads. The stalks were once crystallized, like angelica, and also boiled and eaten as a vegetable, but most modern palates would find the taste unacceptable.

A rich, loamy moisture-retentive soil suits lovage best. Seed can be sown in spring, but buying a young plant from a garden centre is quicker and easier. Once established, it will supply more than enough leaves for a single family. Keep it well watered in dry weather, and lift and divide it every few years, discarding the worn-out centre.

Lovage
*Levisticum officinale*

# MARJORAM

There are three sorts of cultivated marjoram, all needing sun, shelter and free-draining soil. Sweet, or knotted, marjoram (*Origanum majorana*) is the most popular. 'Sweet' refers to its relatively delicate flavour and 'knotted' refers to the tight clusters of tiny white or pink flowers.

Though perennial, it is usually treated as a half-hardy annual in temperate climates. Sow under glass in mid-spring, then plant out after the last frost, spaced 15cm (6in) apart. Keep the seedlings weeded and watered, and pinch out the growing tips when 10cm (4in) high to encourage sideshoots to form.

Pot marjoram (*O. onites*) is a hardy herbaceous perennial, up to 45cm (18in) high. It is easier to buy a young plant than to grow it from seed. Its leaves are smaller than sweet marjoram, and its flowers pinky mauve. In autumn, the above-ground growth should be cut down and the roots protected from frost with a layer of straw or compost. Pot marjoram is a good choice for container-growing.

The golden form of wild, or common, marjoram (*O. vulgare* 'Aureum') is usually sold as an ornamental plant, but its leaves are equally useful in the kitchen. It is a sprawling, carpet-forming plant, shy of flowering. Its leaves turn green as the season progresses. Both it and pot marjoram can be lifted and divided in early spring, or propagated from cuttings in spring or summer.

Marjoram can be dried, a process which intensifies its flavour and aroma, so use sparingly. An essential herb in Italian cooking, marjoram is useful for flavouring meat, poultry and fish dishes; and in salads, soups and stuffings.

Marjoram
*Origanum majorana*

# MINT

There are many types of mint, with different leaf shapes and colours, and subtly different flavours and aromas. All are

Mint
*Mentha spicata*

Apple mint
*M. rotundifolia*

moisture and sun-loving herbaceous perennials, preferring rich soil to support their rapid and somewhat rank growth. They do tolerate poor, dry soil and light shade, though may be stunted as a result.

Mint can be grown from seed but it is quicker and easier to buy a young plant. Mint spreads quickly by means of underground roots; traditional methods of controlling the spread include growing mint in buckets, old sinks or chimney pots sunk into the ground, and sinking sheets of corrugated iron, rigid plastic or polythene vertically into the ground to completely encircle the plant's roots. Renew mint by lifting and dividing every few years.

Most mints grow to a height and spread of 45-60cm (18-24in). The most popular mint is curly-leaved spearmint, *Mentha spicata*, with pointed, bright-green toothed leaves. Variegated apple mint, *M. rotundifolia* 'Variegata' has pretty, grey-green round leaves splashed with white; its scent is a mixture of mint and apple. Bowles mint is a hybrid with woolly, round grey leaves, very popular with cooks.

Mint sauce and mint jelly are traditionally served with roast lamb; mint with peas or new potatoes is an early-summer delight. The leaves can be used fresh as a garnish, or crystallized to decorate cakes and puddings. Mint can be frozen or dried; dried mint has a very concentrated flavour.

# NASTURTIUM

A hardy annual, nasturtium (*Tropaeolum majus*) is more often seen in the ornamental garden than the vegetable or herb garden. Its round, grey-green leaves and single, semi-double or double flowers, ranging in colour from creamy yellow to deepest orange and scarlet, enliven hanging baskets, window boxes, dry, sunny banks and mixed borders. As well as the old-fashioned climbing forms, 1.8m (6ft) high, there are smaller growing bush and dwarf forms.

Nasturtium is included in this book because its peppery leaves can be included in salads, particularly those made of the more tasteless varieties of lettuce. The flowers, which are less strongly flavoured, can also be eaten – indeed, they are sold in the salad section of major food stores. The tubular shape of the flower is perfect for filling with a soft cream cheese as an unusual canapé or appetizer. The flower buds and unripe seeds were traditionally pickled and used as substitutes for capers.

Sow seed 15mm (½in) deep in mid-spring, where the plants are to grow, spaced 25cm (10in) apart. Except for keeping weeds down until the seedlings themselves take over, there is little work required. Removing the faded flowers ensures a continuous supply of blossom, though the seed production suffers accordingly, which is worth keeping in mind if you intend to pickle the seed.

Nasturtiums and insects have a curious relationship. Many gardeners grow nasturtiums as companion plants, as their strong scent is said to repel certain insects. Blackfly, however, find nasturtium irresistible, especially the growing tips. Pinch off and destroy heavily infested tips.

Nasturtium
*Tropaeolum majus*

# PARSLEY

Parsley (*Petroselinium crispum*) is the most popular herb and can be sprinkled over virtually any savoury dish. The obligatory sprig of fresh parsley is used to garnish everything from pre-packed airline food to meals in elegant restaurants. There are several varieties, ranging in height from 20 to 60cm (8 to 24in), and with foliage which is either plain or attractively curled. The latter is often called moss-curled or fern-leafed parsley and makes a pretty edging plant for a herb garden. It can also be used as a substitute for more conventional foliage in a flower arrangement.

Parsley is by nature a biennial, flowering in its second growing season, then dying. It can, however, be treated as an annual and replaced from seed every spring. If its flowering stem is pinched off, it will behave like a perennial; older plants tend to produce tougher leaves, though, and are best replaced.

Choose a rich, moisture-retentive soil and a lightly shaded site for parsley. Sow in mid-spring, then cover with 15mm (½in) of soil. Germination can take up to eight weeks; the colder the soil, the longer the wait. Keep the seedlings weeded and well watered, and thin to 20cm (8in) apart when they are large enough to handle. Parsley tends to bolt if the soil is dry, so water generously in dry spells.

For winter crops of parsley sow seed in late summer, choosing a sunny, sheltered site. Covering the plants in mid-autumn with a layer of straw or cloches helps ensure a continuous supply.

Parsley is an essential ingredient of *bouquet garni* and *fines herbes*, parsley sauce and parsley soup. Though parsley can be dried, the grey-green flakes bear little resemblance in colour, texture or flavour to the real thing. Many purists, faced with dried parsley, would prefer no parsley at all.

Parsley
*Petroselinium crispum*

# ROSEMARY

on vinegar
in these
or frozen
y as a
d fresh

seed; it is
an
inferior

Rosemary (*Rosmarinus officinalis*), indispensable to the cook and attractive in the garden, is another semi-hardy evergreen herb, benefiting from sun, shelter and a free-draining soil. Although it can

Rosemary
*Rosemarinus officinalis*

reach a height of 1.8m (6ft) or more and may need staking, it is usually seen less than half this height. Pruning is confined to cutting out in mid-spring any straggly shoots and wood killed by frost. Very old rosemaries form thick, woody trunks like tiny trees, but they can be cut back by up to half.

Young plants can be bought from a garden centre and planted from mid-spring to late summer. (Those planted in autumn and winter have a higher fatality rate.) Rosemary is also easily propagated from cuttings, and sprigs bought in summer from a greengrocer or supermarket will root. Remove the leaves from the bottom third of the stems, dip in hormone rooting powder, then insert the bare stems around the edge of a small pot filled with a mixture of coarse sand and peat. Keep lightly watered and over-winter in a cool, sunny spot. The following spring, plant as above. (In cold or exposed gardens, grow rosemary against a south- or west-facing wall. Alternatively, grow rosemary in a pot and bring it indoors for the winter.)

The ordinary rosemary has very pretty, pale-blue flowers in early summer. The form 'Albus' has white flowers, the form 'Majorca Pink' has lilac-pink flowers, and the form 'Severn Sea' has intense blue flowers. The slightly more tender, mat-forming rosemary, *R.o.* 'Prostratus', is lovely grown over a wall.

# SAGE

Sage (*Salvia officinalis*) is an old-fashioned, semi-evergreen herb, variously described as a shrub, sub-shrub or perennial. It is very vulnerable to cold, wet winters, and also tends to become less attractive with age, so common practice is to renew plants every three or four years. Cuttings taken in summer root easily, and some gardeners automatically take cuttings against the possibility of winter losses. Sage can be grown from seed, but it is a slow process and not worth the trouble.

A single plant will provide enough leaves for ordinary kitchen use, but since it is a pretty plant a group of three or five would enhance a mixed border. Common sage has grey-green leaves and blue flowers in summer; the form 'Icterina' has yellow-variegated leaves, 'Purpurescens' has purple shoots, and 'Tricolor' has leaves splashed with grey-green, white, pink and purple. All make rounded plants 30-60cm (1-2ft) high, occasionally larger. Named forms, though, are less robust and shyer to flower than the species.

Plant in mid- or late spring in a sunny, sheltered spot with free-draining soil. The leaves can be picked any time of year, though they are more tender before the flowers appear.

The flowers attract bees; more harmful insects, such as cabbage whites and carrot flies, are said to be repelled by sage's strong aroma.

Fresh or dried, sage is the traditional herb to complement poultry, pork sausages and other rich meats, and it is used in sage Derby cheese.

Sage
*Salvia officinalis*

*S. officinalis*
'Purpurescens'

# PARSLEY

Parsley (*Petroselinium crispum*) is the most popular herb and can be sprinkled over virtually any savoury dish. The obligatory sprig of fresh parsley is used to garnish everything from pre-packed airline food to meals in elegant restaurants. There are several varieties, ranging in height from 20 to 60cm (8 to 24in), and with foliage which is either plain or attractively curled. The latter is often called moss-curled or fern-leafed parsley and makes a pretty edging plant for a herb garden. It can also be used as a substitute for more conventional foliage in a flower arrangement.

Parsley is by nature a biennial, flowering in its second growing season, then dying. It can, however, be treated as an annual and replaced from seed every spring. If its flowering stem is pinched off, it will behave like a perennial; older plants tend to produce tougher leaves, though, and are best replaced.

Choose a rich, moisture-retentive soil and a lightly shaded site for parsley. Sow in mid-spring, then cover with 15mm (½in) of soil. Germination can take up to eight weeks; the colder the soil, the longer the wait. Keep the seedlings weeded and well watered, and thin to 20cm (8in) apart when they are large enough to handle. Parsley tends to bolt if the soil is dry, so water generously in dry spells.

For winter crops of parsley sow seed in late summer, choosing a sunny, sheltered site. Covering the plants in mid-autumn with a layer of straw or cloches helps ensure a continuous supply.

Parsley is an essential ingredient of *bouquet garni* and *fines herbes*, parsley sauce and parsley soup. Though parsley can be dried, the grey-green flakes bear little resemblance in colour, texture or flavour to the real thing. Many purists, faced with dried parsley, would prefer no parsley at all.

Parsley
*Petroselinium crispum*

# NASTURTIUM

A hardy annual, nasturtium (*Tropaeolum majus*) is more often seen in the ornamental garden than the vegetable or herb garden. Its round, grey-green leaves and single, semi-double or double flowers, ranging in colour from creamy yellow to deepest orange and scarlet, enliven hanging baskets, window boxes, dry, sunny banks and mixed borders. As well as the old-fashioned climbing forms, 1.8m (6ft) high, there are smaller growing bush and dwarf forms.

Nasturtium is included in this book because its peppery leaves can be included in salads, particularly those made of the more tasteless varieties of lettuce. The flowers, which are less strongly flavoured, can also be eaten – indeed, they are sold in the salad section of major food stores. The tubular shape of the flower is perfect for filling with a soft cream cheese as an unusual canapé or appetizer. The flower buds and unripe seeds were traditionally pickled and used as substitutes for capers.

Sow seed 15mm (½in) deep in mid-spring, where the plants are to grow, spaced 25cm (10in) apart. Except for keeping weeds down until the seedlings themselves take over, there is little work required. Removing the faded flowers ensures a continuous supply of blossom, though the seed production suffers accordingly, which is worth keeping in mind if you intend to pickle the seed.

Nasturtiums and insects have a curious relationship. Many gardeners grow nasturtiums as companion plants, as their strong scent is said to repel certain insects. Blackfly, however, find nasturtium irresistible, especially the growing tips. Pinch off and destroy heavily infested tips.

Nasturtium
*Tropaeolum majus*

# THYME

Being Mediterranean in origin, common thyme (*Thymus vulgaris*) is particularly nice with such dishes as ratatouille, vegetables à la grecque and

Thyme
*Thymus vulgaris*

*T. × citriodorus*
'Aureus'

piperade. Use its powerful flavour and aroma more conventionally to enhance soups and stews, and meat, fish and poultry dishes. A little thyme goes a long way; and dried thyme should be used even more sparingly.

Common thyme forms a wide-spreading evergreen shrub, up to 30cm (12in) high. Buy a young plant and set out in mid- or late spring, in a sunny, sheltered spot with free-draining, poorish soil. For the best flavour, plants should be clipped in spring to prevent flowering. For a prettier garden, and a wealth of bees, clip thyme immediately after flowering to keep it from becoming straggly. Every three or four years, lift and divide thyme to keep it vigorous. Plants can also be propagated from cuttings taken in spring or summer, and, slowest of all, from seed.

There are several thymes from which to choose, some more ornamental than others. Lemon thyme (*T. × citriodorus*) has a lovely lemony scent; it is available in a golden-leaved form, 'Aureus', and a silver-variegated form, 'Silver Queen'. Caraway thyme (*T. herba-barona*) is caraway scented, and wild or creeping thyme (*T. serpyllum*) is a creeping plant traditionally used to make herb paths and lawns. There are many named cultivars, with flowers varying from white to deep, rich crimson.

# PESTS AND DISEASES

Far more things can theoretically go wrong with a vegetable garden than actually do, and the best defence against pests and diseases is a healthy plant. This means one grown in well prepared soil and spacious conditions, with the right amount of food and water. (Small gardens with mixed crops grown in rotation are less vulnerable to huge epidemics than those grown as monocultures, with hundreds of acres of a single crop.)

Before reaching for a spray gun, look at your garden. Rubbish heaps, odds and ends of crops left in the ground after harvest, and weeds that serve as alternative host plants to pests and diseases encourage problems. So do dirty seed trays, pots and stakes, and bringing garden soil into the greenhouse.

## Pests

Unless certain pests have been troublesome in previous years, using pesticides as a preventive isn't a good idea. It is expensive and can result in pests developing a resistance to those chemicals. On the other hand, as soon as a problem declares itself you must act; delaying even a day or two can be disastrous. (Fungicides are often applied as a preventive.)

Always make sure the chemical is right for both the problem and the crop, and use it according to the manufacturer's instructions. *Never* exceed the recommended strength. If it is a spray, choose a windless day, and coat both sides of the leaves, as many insects prefer the undersides. All chemicals are potentially dangerous, and should be stored in clearly marked containers out of reach of children. (Never use containers that once held drinks.) Wash your hands and all equipment thoroughly after each use.

If a plant is badly infested or diseased, it is unlikely to recover and should be destroyed before the problem spreads.

Some pests, like the asparagus beetle, are extremely particular, while others, like aphids and earwigs, attack almost anything. 'Aphids' is an all-embracing term for greenfly, blackfly, root aphids, and 'specialist' aphids, such as cabbage aphids. Aphids are particularly dangerous because they transmit viruses from one plant to another. They are most effectively controlled by systemic insecticides, which are absorbed into a plant's sap so are long lasting in their effectiveness.

'Generalist' soil pests include leatherjackets, millipedes and woodlice, as well as slugs; all are controllable with metaldehyde or methiocarb. Bromophos keeps two particularly ugly soil pests – chafer grubs and cutworms – at bay, as well as a host of 'specialist' soil pests.

If you are wary of chemicals, there are other options. Shallow bowls, filled with beer, diluted milk or sugar-water, can be sunk up to their rims in soil. The slugs are attracted to the liquid and drown. A simpler method is to scatter pieces of orange peel or cabbage leaves in the evening – slugs are most active at night – then collect and burn them the following morning. The Victorians used to organize nocturnal slug hunts, spearing the creatures on long hat pins.

Biological control – using natural predators – is partially effective in the garden. Ladybird larva and adults eat vast quantities of cabbage aphids, though never enough to maintain complete control. Birds, too, help rid a garden of insect pests, but it is hard to attract birds selectively, while at the same time discouraging pigeons, sparrows, bullfinches and other destructive species.

A particularly sophisticated form of biological control can be used in the greenhouse. The predatory mite *Phytoseiulus perimilis* can be introduced to feed on red spider mite. There is also a parasitic wasp, *Encarsia formosa*, which preys upon greenhouse whitefly. Both are available from specialist suppliers and should be introduced as soon as the pests are seen. (Greenhouse biological controls cannot be used preventively, as the predators die if they have no prey to feed on.) Re-introduction during the course of a single season may be necessary.

Companion planting – the growing of certain plants next to one another for a beneficial purpose – is an old idea, but one that is gaining ground again. Most highly aromatic herbs serve, to a certain degree, as insect repellants. Insects have a specialized sense of smell – carrot fly, for example, can pick up the scent of carrot foliage some distance away – and more powerful, or conflicting odours confuse them. Basil is often grown next to tomatoes to keep whitefly away, and savory grown next to broad beans to keep blackfly away. (Interestingly these combinations work equally well in the kitchen.) Nearby rows of chives, onions and parsley are said to protect carrots.

Unless you are squeamish, there is something very satisfying about picking off insects by hand. Caterpillars that are large enough to pick individually, or greenfly totally covering the young shoots of a plant, can be removed en masse and destroyed. Again, check the undersides of the leaves as well. Regular hand picking can often reduce, or even eliminate, the need for chemicals.

If you have to use chemicals, some are less harmful to beneficial insects and wildlife than others. Pyrethrum and nicotine sprays and fumigants are among the safest from that point of view. Malathion, bioresmethrin and derris-based insecticides are also effective without killing indiscriminately, though derris should not be used near ornamental fish ponds as it is lethal to fish. Purists sometimes use soft soap (not caustic soda) diluted with water as a spray. Some insecticides are effective after a single application, though in the case of severe infestations a second application is required. Others, such as derris, normally need several applications to be effective. Again, do what it says on the label.

While no one likes his or her crops decimated, it is important to keep pests in perspective. The occasional nibbled leaf is inevitable in home grown vegetables; perfection is the realm of the commercial grower, the exhibitor, and the food photographer.

## Diseases

Like pests, there are certain diseases that are particular to single plants, and others that attack garden crops indiscriminately. All seedlings started under glass are vulnerable to damping off; they collapse at soil level and die. The fungus is most lethal in overcrowded, damp, close conditions, and unsterilized compost. At the first sign of infection, remove and destroy infected plants and spray the remainder with Cheshunt Compound, zineb or captan.

Grey mould is another promiscuous fungus, which can be found on any above-ground part of a plant.

Worst in cool, damp conditions, indoors and out, and in unventilated greenhouses, grey mould is best dealt with by burning badly infected plants, and spraying the rest with benomyl or thiram.

There are various mildews. Cool, wet springs and autumns encourage downy mildew, which shows up as a yellow discoloration on the leaves, with furry growth underneath. Treatment varies according to the crop; zineb, Bordeaux powder and thiram are the usual fungicides, but make sure you match the fungicide to the crop. Powdery mildew prefers hot, dry summers, and its white coating can be found on leaves and shoots. Young shoots are usually infected first. Pick off and burn infected bits, and destroy badly infected plants. Spray the remainder with benomyl or dinocap.

With both insecticides and fungicides, follow the manufacturer's recommended lapse of time between using and harvesting. This varies from same day harvesting to two weeks or more.

# CALENDAR

**Note:** a seasonal, rather than a month-by-month guide is provided since the weather may vary considerably from year to year and in different areas.

## MIDWINTER

**Dig over** and enrich land (weather permitting)
**Force** chicory, rhubarb, seakale
**Blanch** endive
**Sow (under cover)** radishes
**Harvest** Brussels sprouts, cabbages, celeriac, celery, chard, Jerusalem artichokes, kale, leeks, parsnips, sprouting broccoli, winter radishes

## LATE WINTER

**Dig over** and enrich land (weather permitting)
**Prepare** seed beds
**Warm up** soil with cloches
**Force** chicory, rhubarb, seakale
**Blanch** endive
**Sow (artificial heat)** aubergines, cauliflowers, celeriac, celery, cucumbers, leeks, onions, peppers, tomatoes
**Sow (under cover)** beetroot, broad beans, Brussels sprouts, cabbages, carrots, cauliflowers, lettuces, onions, radishes, peas, spinach, turnips
**Sow (outdoors)** parsnips
**Chit** potatoes
**Plant** Jerusalem artichokes

**Harvest** Brussels sprouts, cabbages, celery, chard, Jerusalem artichokes, kale, leeks, parsnips, sprouting broccoli, winter radishes

## EARLY SPRING

**Prepare** seed beds
**Warm up** soil with cloches
**Sow (artificial heat)** aubergines, cauliflowers, cucumbers, celeriac, peppers, pumpkins, tomatoes
**Sow (under cover)** cauliflowers, carrots, celeriac, celery, leeks, lettuces, peas, radishes
**Sow (outdoors)** beetroot, broad beans, Brussels sprouts, cabbages, carrots, calabrese, corn salad, Good King Henry, Hamburg parsley, kohl rabi, lettuces, leeks, onions, parsnips, peas, radishes, salsify, scorzonera, sorrel, spinach, turnips
**Plant** asparagus, cabbages, cauliflowers, globe artichokes, Jerusalem artichokes, lettuces, onion sets, potatoes, rhubarb, seakale, shallots
**Harvest** Brussels sprouts, cabbages, celeriac, chard, kale, leeks, parsnips, rhubarb, sorrel, sprouting broccoli, winter radishes

## MID-SPRING

**Warm up** soil with cloches
**Weed and water** crops as necessary
**Mulch** crops outdoors

**Clear** remaining brassica stumps
**Sow (under cover)** aubergines, celeriac, celery, cucumbers, French beans, marrows, pumpkins, New Zealand spinach, peppers, runner beans, sweetcorn, tomatoes
**Sow (outdoors)** beetroot, broad beans, Brussels sprouts, cabbages, Chinese cabbages, calabrese, carrots, cauliflowers, chard, dandelions, endive, Florence fennel, French beans, Hamburg parsley, kale, kohl rabi, leeks, lettuces, onions, peas, radishes, runner beans, salsify, scorzonera, sprouting broccoli, sorrel, spinach, turnips
**Plant** asparagus, Brussels sprouts, cabbages, cauliflowers, lettuces, onion sets, potatoes, seakale
**Harvest** asparagus, cabbages, cauliflowers, chard, Good King Henry, kale, lettuces, radishes, rhubarb, sprouting broccoli, seakale

## LATE SPRING

**Weed and water** crops as necessary
**Mulch** crops outdoors
**Sow (under cover)** cucumbers, pumpkins, marrows
**Sow (outdoors)** asparagus peas, beetroot, Brussels sprouts, cabbages, calabrese, cardoons, carrots, cauliflowers, chard, chicory, Chinese cabbage, endive, Florence fennel, kohl rabi, land cress, lettuces, mangetout, onions, peas, radishes, salsify, scorzonera, spinach, swedes, turnips

**Plant (with protection)** cucumbers, marrows, pumpkins, sweetcorn, tomatoes
**Plant** Brussels sprouts, cabbages, cauliflowers, celeriac, celery, French beans, leeks, potatoes, runner beans
**Harvest** asparagus, sprouting broccoli, cabbages, chard, Good King Henry, lettuces, radishes, rhubarb, sorrel, spring onions, turnips, watercress, winter cauliflowers

## EARLY SUMMER

**Weed and water** crops as necessary
**Stake and support** as necessary
**Sow (outdoors)** beetroot, calabrese, carrots, chard, chicory, Chinese cabbages, endive, Florence fennel, kohl rabi, land cress, lettuces, marrows, New Zealand spinach, peas, radishes, spinach, spring onions, swedes, turnips
**Plant** aubergines, Brussels sprouts, sprouting broccoli, cabbages, cauliflowers, celeriac, celery, French beans, leeks, marrows, peppers, pumpkins, tomatoes, sweetcorn
**Harvest** asparagus, beetroot, broad beans, cabbages, calabrese, carrots, French beans, cauliflowers, chard, cucumbers, French beans, Good King Henry, kohl rabi, lettuces, onions, peas, potatoes, rhubarb, sorrel, spinach, spring onions, turnips, watercress

# CALENDAR

## MIDSUMMER

**Weed and water** crops as necessary
**Stake and support** as necessary
**Sow (outdoors)** beetroot, cabbages, carrots, chard, chicory, Chinese cabbages, corn salad, endive, Florence fennel, kohl rabi, land cress, lettuces, spring onions, peas, radishes (summer and winter), spinach, turnips
**Plant** Brussels sprouts, cabbages, calabrese, cauliflowers, kale, leeks, sprouting broccoli
**Harvest** asparagus, aubergines, beetroot, broad beans, calabrese, carrots, celery, chard, courgettes, cucumbers, endive, Florence fennel, French beans, globe artichokes, leeks, lettuces, marrows, onions, peas, peppers, potatoes, radishes, runner beans, shallots, spinach, spring onions, sweetcorn, tomatoes, turnips, watercress

## LATE SUMMER

**Weed and water** crops as necessary
**Stake and support** as necessary
**Sow (outdoors)** beetroot, cabbages, carrots, chard, Chinese cabbages, corn salad, endive, Florence fennel, kohl rabi, land cress, lettuces, onions, radishes (summer and winter), spinach, spring onions
**Plant** cabbages, cauliflowers, kale, leeks, sprouting broccoli
**Harvest** asparagus peas, aubergines, beetroot, broad beans, cabbages, calabrese, carrots, celery, chard, Chinese cabbages, courgettes, cucumbers, endive, French beans, kohl rabi, land cress, leeks, lettuces, marrows, onions, peas, peppers, potatoes, radishes, runner beans, shallots, sorrel, spinach, spring onions, sweetcorn, tomatoes, turnips, watercress

## EARLY AUTUMN

**Weed and water** crops as necessary
**Stake and support** as necessary, including earthing up of winter brassicas
**Protect** with cloches late sowings of salad vegetables and dwarf beans
**Sow (outdoors)** cabbages, endive, lettuces, radishes, spinach, turnips
**Plant** cabbages, lettuces
**Harvest** asparagus peas, aubergines, beetroot, broad beans, cabbages, calabrese, carrots, celery, chard, chicory, Chinese cabbages, courgettes, cucumbers, endive, Florence fennel, French beans, kohl rabi, lettuces, leeks, marrows, onions, peas, peppers, potatoes, radishes, shallots, sorrel, spinach, sweetcorn, tomatoes, turnips

## MID-AUTUMN

**Protect with cloches** late sowings of salad vegetables and dwarf beans
**Clear ground** of frost-tender summer vegetables
**Cut down** asparagus, globe artichokes, Jerusalem artichokes

**Lift and store** root vegetables
**Blanch** endive
**Sow** broad beans, cauliflowers, lettuces, peas
**Plant** chard, cabbages
**Harvest** asparagus peas, beetroot, Brussels sprouts, cabbages, cardoons, carrots, cauliflowers, celeriac, celery, chard, chicory, Chinese cabbages, corn salad, cucumbers, French beans, Hamburg parsley, Jerusalem artichokes, kohl rabi, leeks, lettuces, parsnips, peas, potatoes, pumpkins, radishes, runner beans, salsify, scorzonera, spinach, swedes, sweetcorn, tomatoes, turnips

## LATE AUTUMN

**Dig over** and enrich land, weather permitting
**Lift** and store root vegetables, or protect from frost those left in ground
**Blanch** dandelions, endive

**Force** chicory, rhubarb, seakale
**Sow (outdoors)** broad beans, peas
**Harvest** Brussels sprouts, cabbages, cauliflowers, celeriac, chard, chicory (non-forcing), Chinese cabbages, corn salad, Hamburg parsley, Jerusalem artichokes, kale, leeks, lettuces, parsnips, salsify, scorzonera, swedes, winter radishes

## EARLY WINTER

**Dig over** and enrich land, weather permitting
**Check** vegetables in store for signs of rot
**Blanch** dandelion, endive
**Force** chicory, rhubarb, seakale
**Harvest** Brussels sprouts, cabbages, chard, chicory (non-forcing), corn salad, Jerusalem artichokes, kale, leeks, parsnips

# GLOSSARY

**Annual** A plant which germinates, flowers and sets seed in one growing season, then dies. Though a spring-to-autumn life cycle is usual, some annuals complete the cycle in three weeks, while hardy annuals are often sown in autumn to over-winter and die the following summer.

**Biennial** A plant which completes its life cycle in two growing seasons. Most vegetable biennials are grown as annuals and harvested before they flower and set seed.

**Blanching** A method of producing pale, tender, leafy growth by excluding light. Celery, leeks, rhubarb, chicory, endive and seakale can be blanched. Blanching is sometimes combined with forcing (q.v.)

**Bolting** The premature production of flowers, before a plant is fully mature. It is often caused by uneven water supplies in hot weather. Lettuces, radishes, beetroot and onions are notorious bolters.

**Calyx** The protective, usually green, outer covering of a flower. A calyx is made of sepals which, in the case of tomatoes, look like tiny leaves.

**Catch crop** Quick-growing vegetables sown on ground temporarily vacant between being used for slower-growing crops. Radish, spinach and lettuce are typical catch crops.

**Compost** Either rotted-down kitchen waste and organic matter from the garden, used as an alternative to well rotted manure; or various loam- or peat-based mixtures used for growing plants in containers.

**Cultivar** See Variety.

**Division** A method of reproduction, by which a plant is separated into several parts, each capable of growth. Perennials, such as sorrel and mint, are divided by their roots; tubers, such as Jerusalem artichokes, can also be divided.

**F₁ hybrid** The first generation of plants resulting from the cross of two species or varieties (q.v.). $F_1$ hybrids are usually more expensive but better quality plants than their parents.

**Forcing** The speeding up of plant growth, usually by applying artificial heat, to obtain early crops. Chicory, seakale and rhubarb are often forced. The process is sometimes combined with blanching (q.v.).

**Green manure** A crop, such as mustard, rape or clover, grown specifically to be dug into the soil to enrich it. The method is more suitable for agricultural-scale crop production than small vegetable patches.

**Hardening off** Acclimatizing plants started in warm conditions indoors to the cooler conditions outdoors: a slow process.

**Hardy** Able to tolerate normal amounts of frost, although some hardy plants are hardier than others. Hardy plants started off in warm conditions are more vulnerable to frost than those grown in harsher conditions.

**Half hardy** These are plants that need protection from frost. Half-hardy vegetables are often sown under glass, then transplanted outdoors after the last frost.

**Intercrop** Quick-growing vegetables sown in rows between slower-growing ones; again, radish, spinach and lettuce are the usual choice.

**Manure** Bulky animal matter, such as dung, or vegetable matter, such as compost, dug into the soil. Manure improves the structure of the soil and supplies nutrients.

**Mulch** A covering of the soil surface to conserve soil moisture, prevent weed growth and, if organic, to enrich the soil and improve its texture. Traditional mulches include well rotted manure, garden compost, lawn clippings, leafmould, spent mushroom compost, straw and peat. Alternatively, black polythene can be used.

**Perennial** A plant which lives for several years after flowering. Rhubarb, globe artichokes and asparagus are perennial vegetables. Tomatoes and runner beans are tender perennials, cultivated as annuals.

**Pinching out** The removal, usually with the thumb and forefinger, of soft, new tip growth. Pinching out encourages bushy growth and the production of side shoots, flowers and fruit.

**Seed dressing** A coating which protects seeds from diseases or pests, or both, according to its contents. Some seeds can be bought already dressed, and dressing is also available for treating non-dressed seeds prior to sowing.

**Set** Potato tubers and onion bulbs specially grown and prepared for planting. Potato sets are taken from virus-free, immature plants and exposed to the air for several days. Onion sets are heat treated, immature bulbs.

**Successional sowing** Sowing a small quantity of seed at set intervals, such as every two weeks, to prolong the harvesting season.

**Variety** A naturally occurring variation within the species. A variety which occurs in a cultivated plant is called a 'cultivar', but the two words are often used interchangeably. (Most vegetable varieties are in fact cultivars.)

# INDEX

# INDEX